NOVEL IDEA!

All you need to know to write & publish your novel *Now!*

With *a Southern twist*

By
Jesse R. (Randy) Hale
&
Candice Lawrence

Shades Creek Press, LLC
Savannah, Georgia

www.shadescreekpress.com

This is a work of non-fiction, and is devised from the experiences and research of the authors. All references to places or locations originate from the authors, their experiences, and travels.

First Edition
First Printing, 2014

Book design by Jesse R. Hale
Cover Concept Design by Jesse R. Hale & Candice Lawrence
Final Cover by Tristin Tungate
Editing by Candice Lawrence and Jesse Hale

NOVEL IDEA!
ISBN: 978-0-9838376-7-1

Printed in the United States of America

Dedication by Jesse R. Hale

This book is dedicated to all those who have a story they want to tell. May you find the courage and stamina to chase your dream, to write and publish your story; to you, I say, *Carpe diem*!

And to my grandchildren, may you each chase and catch your dreams! Dream BIG! Always think *positive*! Always <u>BELIEVE</u> in the power of your *dreams*! And don't ever let anybody hold you back or tell you that you can't achieve your dreams! Dreaming about what seems impossible or improbable is what motivates a person to make a different life for him or herself. You are each special and unique, and I am very proud of each one of you! Work hard, stay focused, and go catch your dream.

Go catch your DREAMS! Pop Loves You!

"If you can dream it, you can do it."
—Walt Disney

"Whatever you can do or dream you can, begin it. Boldness has genius, power and magic in it!"
—Johann Wolfgang von Goethe

"Magic is believing in yourself, if you can do that, you can make anything happen."
—Johann Wolfgang von Goethe

Dedication by Candice Lawrence

To my family: Jonathan, for constantly igniting my imagination (even still), showing me at a young age that reading really can be fun, and that the best big brothers *always* have time to read to their illiterate little sisters. Mommy and Daddy, for challenging, supporting, and encouraging me—whether it was softball, pre-algebra, music, or writing, you never doubted my potential; here's to reading everything from bedtime stories to full-length novels to and with me, our summer library visits, and the made-up stories. I'm blessed for all you've done and I hope this book mirrors the inspiration I find in each of you.

Topics Include:

1. Getting Started with Your Writing
2. Your Writing Space and Schedule
3. Outlining vs. Scene Sketching
4. The Story Concept
5. Point of View, You Choose
6. Setting and Place
7. Predetermined Outcome or Organic Emerging Story
8. Using Humor and Satire in Writing
9. The Art and Science of Writing Consistently
10. The Art of Dialogue & Southern Dialect
11. Finding Inspiration
12. Circles of Support and Encouragement
13. Plot Development
14. Characters: Protagonist, Antagonist, Supporting
15. Believe in your Story: It's Your Creation and You're the Expert
16. Celebrate Your Writing Goals
17. The Editing and Proofreading Process
18. The Art of Writing a Good Sentence!
19. Using Conflict and Suspense to Hook the Reader
20. POD Publishing vs. the Traditional Route
21. Marketing your Book
22. Setting up an LLC for Writing, Publishing and Marketing Your Book
23. A Final Word.

Novel Idea!

Thoughts about writing and creating art through the narrative:

You need not expect to get your book right the first time. Go to work and revamp or rewrite it. God only exhibits His thunder and lightning at intervals, and so they always command attention. These are God's adjectives. You thunder and lightning too much; the reader ceases to get under the bed, by and by.

- Letter to Orion Clemens, 23 March 1878

Let us guess that whenever we read a sentence & like it, we unconsciously store it away in our model-chamber; & it goes, with the myriad of its fellows, to the building, brick by brick, of the eventual edifice which we call our style.

- Letter to George Bainton, 15 Oct 1888

The act of writing is the creation from the portal to one's heart and soul; the magic of writing is allowing others to peer through it and experience the mystical journey through the caverns of the mind.

Jesse R. Hale

Introduction

Every good book must have a good, strong first chapter, one that teases the reader and lures the prospective co-conspirator of the imagination to flip the pages and continue to read. The reader, your traveling companion on this journey of make believe, requires of you the fare of constant suspense, intrigue, fantasy, and humor or sarcasm, or both. This book of prose and tell-tale stories, plot twists and turns, framed in whatever contextual reference you choose to construct, must capture the allure of a time and place imagined away from the realities of one's present world. Otherwise, why does one read fiction?

"The way to get started is to quit talking and begin doing."

—Walt Disney

Chapter 1

Getting Started with Your Writing

If you're reading this book, either as an e-book or a soft-cover edition, I offer my congratulations. You are now on your way to fulfilling perhaps your life-long dream!

I want to congratulate you on taking the first step toward accomplishing your goal of writing a novel, or a book. You may be one of many who harbors a story or an idea for a book, but who lack the knowledge or self-confidence to begin the writing process. Remember this, as you begin the writing process, you are the expert on your topic as you see it and as you describe it through your prose and narrative. Whether your idea is for a fictional novel or a non-fiction piece on a specific subject, YOU are the expert through your perspective, your opinion and experiences. As Mark Twain once famously said, "Do not argue with stupid people, they will drag you down to their level and beat you with their experience."

And to quote Tom Clancey, who recently passed from the this world at the young age of 67, and who once told a room full of military personnel at a writers conference, "If you want to write a book, get a computer, sit down and write. Do it! You can do it. It's not as hard as you think."

Little did I know that Tom Clancey wrote his book, *Hunt for Red October,* which won him notoriety and fame, was written as a part time project as he worked as an insurance agent. Once the book was completed, it was promptly rejected by the traditional publishing confabs in New York and elsewhere. He published his book, *Hunt for Red October,* through a military press. It quickly won the praises of military readers around the world, as well as from President Reagan, who invited Clancey to dine and lunch at the Whitehouse on numerous occasions. Needless to say, Clancey gave up selling insurance soon afterwards. My obvious point here is that the "traditional" way or route of publishing a book, albeit still the crème de la crème, is not the only way to achieve your dream of publishing your book.

As we go forward, I will reference other authors' works, articles, magazine sources, etc. You should begin building your collection of ideas for writing, your notes about your subject, and a basic sketch about your book idea now. This can be an outline, a list of sections or chapters, or a sequential list of events, places, characters, or timeframes related to your subject area, your story.

Now, let's talk about how to get started.

As a writer (and you need to begin thinking of yourself in that way, kind of like being a teacher although you might not have a teaching job yet), you will need to think through the whole idea and process of writing. Writing is a mechanical process, and has rules for grammar, sentence structure, voice or "point of view," not to mention the variations of the characters in your story. But as the creator of this piece, you have to think through each part, much like picking apart each scene of a play. In fact, your writing should become a mental motion picture in your mind. Play out each scene. Soon, you will notice that your inner thoughts will begin to shift from one character to another as you mentally act out each conversation or dialogue.

There is also the *act of writing*, which we'll get into more later, but suffice to say that it is a mental mindset that you must be able to manipulate and adjust in order to actually produce writing, no matter how good it is or if you rip it up and start over, you have to actually put your thoughts on paper. It is stated many places by many writers and editors, if you want to be a writer, you have to write...so, write!

You may find yourself staring at the computer screen, or the yellow writing pad, or at the walls, wrestling with how to start, what words to use, what sentence to write first. The trick is to just write something, it will begin to flow. It seems to me, especially in the beginning, the harder you think about how to get started with your story, the more difficult it is. Conversely, when you just relax and tell your story, or lay out the argument for your case, or describe an event, it flows. It's the act of transferring what you are thinking about onto the piece of paper or onto the computer screen. Don't worry about what others might think about it; just write it!

I have a good friend with whom I worked many years ago. She was the registrar at one of the high schools where I worked, and we became instant friends. She was like a big sister and quickly became a close comrade. She told me recently that she was working on a book about her grandmother's childhood. She described to me that she had recorded hours and hours of her grandmother recounting the stories of growing up in the mountains of north Georgia, living near Native American people and of her grandmother having listened to her grandparents tell stories of fighting in the Civil War, or what some refer to as the *War of Northern Aggression*. My friend has hours and hours of wonderful stories.

The trick is to get them down on paper into a readable form that will hold the audience's interest. The story has to be compelling and interesting. And it must connect emotionally with the reader. But the first thing is to get it on paper. The details of what you are trying to write or create will reveal the story. It may even reveal an unintended story. If this happens, then you will know that you have hit that strata, or zone, of writing where the story you are creating takes on a life of its own. As you begin your writing, be aware that the story will lead you down roads you could not have predicted. Perhaps the plot will develop in ways that you had not thought about, and characters will emerge from the story in surprising ways. Perhaps you may begin your writing project with the ending in mind, but then be sideswiped and taken hostage by the story itself in ways that were totally unpredictable at the point when you wrote the first sentence. Let the story guide you.

As Lawrence Block once wrote in his version of a book about writing a novel, which I also recommend, a writer may have several copies of the first 100 pages of books started only to die a certain death of the lack of sustained longevity, but the one book, the one manuscript catches fire and takes on its own persona. This point made by Lawrence Bock is well taken, and illustrates accurately the probable course of your upcoming experiences as a writer.

Chapter 2

Your Writing Space and Schedule

A lot of people who are writers or who claim to be writers will say that you need to have your own space when approaching a writing project. And, indeed, there is an advantage. There are books upon books that you can purchase at your local Barnes & Noble, all on the subject of finding your "writing space" in order to connect with your inner self and like a projectile, blast yourself into the writing zone.

All of that is nice, but here's the bare-bones truth. You will have to do a self-assessment, however you deem to accomplish this task, on what situational environment will be necessary in order for you to focus and concentrate on your writing. If you're the distractible type, then just know that you will need a space and schedule for writing that is deemed your holy ground, or area, not to be disturbed. If this describes you, then you can't write in the middle of kids fighting over who's watching what show on television, or whose time it is to have someone come over to play, etc. Or, people asking you a thousand times what you're writing or working on. You, my friend, must reclaim a space all your own as your "writer's cave."

One of the aspects of writing that interests me a lot is how other writers actually accomplish the task of thinking through ideas, plots, characters, information, and then actually finding the rhythm of putting it down on paper, as it were. Stephen King has written a book on writing titled, *On Writing,* which I highly recommend, by the way. In his book, he describes his writing space. He has a farm in Maine, and he travels there to find inspiration and solace from the daily world, and to create his fantastic stories, plots, and suspense.

David McCullough, who is a renowned author and journalist, has an old and small cabin. Much like Thoreau who had a cabin in Walden Woods, McCullough locks himself away from the daily routines of his world, and plunges into the world around his topic or subject for which he is writing. I have seen him interviewed several times where he described how he uses an old Royal typewriter. McCullough explained that using an old non-electric pewriter forced him to go more slowly and to be re methodical and thoughtful with his writing.

William Faulkner, who won the Pulitzer Prize riting, worked at all hours of the night, in a room of his house in Mississippi. Hemingway n 100 different places all over the world, and included some details of his writing ent into the story he was working on. Carl who lived and worked in an area just ndersonville, North Carolina, would spend ven days in an upstairs area of the attic that he converted to his own personal and private writing world. Every room of his house is filled with books stacked from ceiling to floor.

In finding or creating your writing space, the one specific advice I'll grant you is this: find a comfortable chair. Your writing chair…and desk or table for that matter, can generate inspiration beyond your recognition. And, there is a book on that.

So, here's the bottom line: Find whatever works for you, and establish a space and routine. Some of the self-proclaimed experts espouse that to become a serious writer, and to accomplish your goal of writing a novel or book within, say, a year, you must write every day, no matter what. I would have to agree with this assertion in theory, and it's certainly a good goal, but the important element to draw from this advice is to just be consistent with your writing. Don't lose your fire!

Chapter 3

Outlining vs. Scene Sketching

Now, this chapter will be fun! My dear high school English teacher, Mrs. Reed, who I admire and respect with the utmost highest regard, might disagree here. The school of thought on the approach to writing has changed and evolved over recent years…say since the Fall of 1974…my senior year.

If you're about my age, 57 at this writing, you were no doubt thrown into the chasms of "outlining" the topics for which you were about to embark on a thoughtful and thought-provoking exercise of writing prescriptively by the detailed and precise outline. Frankly, I found this exercise excruciatingly difficult, and I floundered greatly as I mustered the courage to first compose an outline that would meet Mrs. Reed's strict parameters, only then to expose an amateurish prose about a topic grabbed from the echoes of my very inexperienced brain, to produce 18 to 25 pages of cohesive narrative.

My high school senior "theme" paper was on comparing and contrasting the aspects of religious belief or non-belief surrounding Theism, Creationism, and Atheism. While I now acknowledge that these three are not exactly parallel, I did with all the bravery I could muster, plow into the act of comparative research. I employed the generosity of the pastor of the church I attended and anyone else who would lend an "official" and thus, creditable opinion. After all, Mrs. Reed had declared in her utmost eloquent southern repose, that a comparison-contrast paper would be the more interesting of senior papers, if you were one who needed an extra edge for a passing grade. I immediately, without public declaration, staked my flag on that approach to my looming writing project…for obvious reasons…my grade needed a boost!

So, as you now prepare for this newly accepted life goal of writing a book, take a minute and wipe the sweat from your forehead. You're not in senior English class. You now have more control and latitude over your creative writing project. If you were like me in senior English class, a square peg that had to somehow fit into a round hole, never fear. Your English teacher may be shocked to hear you're writing a book, but he or she will be proud, no less! So, proceed with pride and courage.

Now, let's get back to the outline. If you're comfortable with Roman Numerals, upper-case letters, and numbers, then carry on. Sketch out your outline and through the series of upper-case letters and numbers, plot your story. But if you're like me, read on.

Another way to plan or layout a story is with a sketch method. Scene-by-scene, each movement, each conversation, each conflict, each mystery can be detailed within the confines of each scene, conversation, or setting. Think about this approach. It actually mirrors our own daily lives as we unfold each hour of each day. Every conversation, every argument, and every encounter records our life history, which in an instant, can be rewound and replayed, over and over again. During these replays, we connect the dots and make some sense of it all, just before we close our eyes and drift off to sleep.

If you think of life's daily dosages of mystery and intrigue, then use this approach to breathe life into your prosaic creation. Draw circles or boxes to separate the various scenes, while leaving space to make copious notes of scene details, and of twists and turns of your narrative enclaves. As you begin to accumulate a reasonable collection of scenes, look for the tantalizing break, a place in the story that will cause the reader to walk out into traffic just to get the page turned for the next chapter, and the rest of the story… Always leave the reader hanging.

To me, and of course this is after some 36 plus years of life after senior English class, but to me, this approach is more telling and offers a higher degree of probable completion with some relative sense of the written piece of narrative prose. Working from an outline, as I recall today, was as artificial as homemade cigars made of rabbit grass and grocery sack paper, rolled up to look like the real thing, nonetheless a Swisher Sweets or King Edwards Cigar. It ignited and smoldered, and we eventually got a draw, but it was no Swisher Sweets or King Edwards! And thus, an outline is not a scene sketch, albeit with the highest respect and pardon to Mrs. Reed, as well as my dear sister, who was by the luck of the draw, my junior English teacher, and who gave me a "C" on a major paper, citing that it was inadequate and fell short of the goal. Still, they tried with great might to guide my efforts along the more traditional means of outlining and writing.

So, the battle of which approach to use is yours to resolve. Try each approach, the *outline* and the *scene-by-scene sketch* for laying out the first chapter. See which one feels more natural, easier to complete, to think through, and which causes you to see your story chapters ahead. Sometimes, you'll find that thoughts and ideas will hit you at the oddest times, like driving down the road or while you're in the shower. As soon as possible, jot your thoughts down, and go back later to fill in the details. I promise that with this exercise of salvaging ideas about your writing project, whether it is a novel, short story, or a non-fiction piece, you will feverishly scribble down the thoughts of your topic that only momentarily popped above the surface of your consciousness, if only for a few seconds, but enough time to write down the gist of your new found experiential vision, and it will not resemble an outline; thus my point.

One other flag of warning: The story in which you're about to embark will change. You must be comfortable with that aspect. Once you begin the writing process and adopt the notion and mindset of being referred to as a writer, your story will take on its own rhythm and cantor. I recommend that you write with pen and paper during your first take on whatever scene you choose for this exercise, and put it away in the back of a desk drawer. Sign and date it, and label it with an inscription that this was your very first creation of your now published book. You'll thank me later.

Chapter 4

The Story Concept!

Everybody has a story! What's yours? Moreover, what story are you attempting to capture to serve as your first official piece of narrative or description...your book?

This will require some "think time," and perhaps even some soul searching. Try narrowing your focus to the top three ideas for which you'd like to write about. Think about whether or not you would have an audience. Would it be interesting? Would it be funny? What books or stories have you read or seen in your research that is similar to yours? How is your story different? What makes your story unique? One of the things I like to do is go to my local Barnes & Noble bookstore and just browse around. If I have an idea, like this book for instance, I will research the topic, and then go see what is currently on the shelves for what I tend to think of as the "public offering" of books that are for sale. I also check both Amazon.com and barnesandnoble.com as to what the hot sellers are. I also conduct a search for similar topics or titles. And while there are many books out there about how to write your first novel, or how to become a writer, etc., I believe that I have a unique enough perspective that my book will be different than any of the others out there.

Once you have thought about and answered these questions, you will be ready to write a preliminary list of chapters or outline a few major headings for potential chapters or sections. The point here is that you may have an idea about what you want to write, but since it probably has only been haunting you for a select number of years, and assuming you haven't attempted this process previously, the facts and boundaries of the potential story have to be tested and filtered. Is there enough to the idea to last 200 - 300 pages, or 70,000 to 100,000 words? Sounds daunting, doesn't it? It is...and isn't! But if you do this right, and if you're persistent, you'll be rewarded for the experience.

Let me make a specific point here!

As you progress through the maze of writing...of producing a book, for which you will soon realize that there are many more critics than there are encouragers, you have to move forward with a "definite purpose," as Napoleon Hill (1936), stated when he wrote the book, *Think and Grow Rich.*

I want to be clear here. You are the expert for your story or book. YOU and only you know how it will end, or what direction it will go. And that is an enormous and fabulous position to be in. You, as the newly crowned *writer,* control the universe that lies between the pages and in the depths of your imagination. It is now time to think inwardly, to find your Muse, that inner soul that has the power to propel you forward. You're a writer. You're a creator of stories and plots and suspense, of tears and joy, of love and lust, of the beginning and the end. Simply, put, it's your story. Go write it. As your story unfolds, it will lead you in the direction of explicit description and creation. It's your story. Own it!

I began my story, which became the book, *Island Castaways,* in the summer of 1994. It was in late August or maybe early September. I had had this burning desire to write a book, to create a story. It was in my head. But, I had just enrolled at Vanderbilt University, the Peabody College of Education in the Educational Leadership program for my doctorate. This was another obsession I had at the time.

I knew that I could not do both. So, I sketched out and wrote the semblance of what would become, at least in part, the first chapter of my book. It would take many years to complete this project. There would be several stops and starts along the way, not to mention all the life experiences of raising a family, pursuing my career, moving a couple of times, building two houses, and finally getting refocused in 2006.

In 2010, I became really serious about completing the book and getting it published. I came very close to finishing the writing, but it was in rough, and I do mean very rough, shape. I had several people read it and comment. Most would not give me the feedback I needed. Finally, I coaxed my wife into reading it and editing the project after the story was completely finished.

In June 2011, my wife and I spent a week in Minicott Beach, North Carolina. We stayed in a century old house on the Niece River. We were there for the purpose of my writing, and her horseback riding lessons. There, with the magic of the river flowing by, and the birds flying around, I had the time to allow my mind to think and contemplate the story. As I delved into each of my character's mind and body, and mentally lived each of their lives, the ending of the book took on a life of its own. The story itself guided me. Each of the character's experiences took my hand and carried me down that gravel road that led from the Victoria House to the town of San Pedro, and to the ship that night as they escape the island. Their emotions became mine. I felt their hurt, their concern, their anxiousness, and finally, their mixture of emotions.

As I began writing the next to last chapter, I suddenly knew the ending. I had not known before that point how the story would end. I found myself filled with excitement, as I could see the ending coming. I couldn't get the words on paper quick enough. I could see where the characters were traveling, and how this experience changed them. It was surreal. The words on the paper seemed to elevate me to the level of an outer body experience. Not only was I finally finishing the book, but I was finishing a long personal journey, one that began in ninth grade, and then was further fueled throughout high school and my early college years as I struggled with my English assignments, and my writing. Many said I could never do it; that I didn't have the skills necessary to write a book, to complete a story. But here I was, on the precipice of completing a BOOK. The feeling was more than elation. It was spiritual. It moved me. But that is what writing...and thus reading a good story should do, move you.

Now, do you understand what you have at your fingertips? I hope so. Stay on course, and I promise, this experience will be awesome!

***The Value of Reading Good Writing*!**

Stephen King, in his book, *On Writing (1997)*, wrote that if you want to be a good writer, and if you want to develop your skills as a good writer, then you should read good works. Among his suggestions were Hemingway, Faulkner, Joyce, Pat Conroy, and many other modern day novelists. King's point here is to read analytically. Study how Hemingway used dialogue to move his sometimes laborious stories forward, how he linked places and events together, as in *Islands in the Stream*, which was the last novel Hemingway wrote, but was not published before his death in 1961. This book was the compilation of three novelettes that he had been working on for several years. He expected this book to catapult him back into the spotlight as the renowned expert novelist. He was credited with radically changing the way in which novels and short stories were written, primarily by his use of exotic details and short precise dialogue that moved his stories from various parts of the world, or through the valleys that lay below the mist of the heights of Mount Kilimanjaro. Hemingway wrote incessantly, about everything and everywhere.

After reading Stephen King's book, I began to immerse myself in Hemingway's work. I wanted to read all of his work. I studied him as a writer. I wanted to understand how he thought and how he approached his writing. I believe that Hemingway, much like Conroy and even Steinbeck, weaved his own personal life story into his work. Certainly, as a writer, we are influenced by our life experiences. I would think that it would be inextricably impossible to separate one's life experience from the written stories produced on paper. Some writers are better at hiding that unavoidable truth, however.

While there are numerous points and details of writing for which the story's direction is set, none is more effective than the point of view the books takes in order to unfold the story.

Chapter 5

Point of View, You Choose!

One of the most famous lines in literature, especially American Southern literature, comes from Margaret Mitchell's masterpiece, *Gone with the Wind,* as so dramatically delivered, "My dear, I don't give a damn." This, my dear friend and reader of this modest how-to book is a declarative example of first person point of view. There's no question or disillusionment of what Rhett meant when he delivered the message to poor Scarlett. Nor did the audience have to wonder, whether they were reading from the printed page or sitting mesmerized in the movie theater.

Here's another way to look at it. Imagine that you're telling or recounting some adventure from which you have just returned. How would you tell it? Would you tell it from a personal experience perspective? Probably. Then, this is "first person." With this approach, the writer will use first person pronouns such as "I" or "me" or "my." The person telling the story will be directly involved in the story and all its details as they unfold. One drawback or limitation with the first person point of view is that the writer can't reveal any hints or clues as to plot suspense. This approach is, however, easier for telling the story.

If you were telling about someone else's experience, where you recount the story details from a "story-teller" perspective or point of view, then, this is considered as "third person" point of view. The third person point of view is a notch up on the challenge meter for young or inexperienced writers, but it can facilitate for the writer many more choices for developing story plot, character details, twists and turns, and if mastered, will lend itself to keeping the reader on the edge of their seats. With this approach, the writer can wonder around inside the main character's head. He can see and hear the main character's inner thoughts, secrets, fears, and feelings of excitement. The writer can reveal anticipated points of story details, as well as how the main character plots and manipulates his or her movements throughout the story. Probably the most challenging approach in storytelling, however, is the third person omniscient.

The third person omniscient point of view is the crème de la crème of points of view in writing. This approach offers the most choices and most flexibility when writing and creating a story where there are numerous characters and subplots. The third person omniscient point of view allows the writer, and thus, the reader, to see inside the minds of multiple characters. The reader becomes enthralled with each story detail, and either wants to cheer on a particular character in a story, or becomes highly agitated and throws the book across the room in anger and in wanting to demolish the antagonist as the story unfolds. Some readers will want to cheer on the coming hero in the story.

While this approach is the most challenging, it can make for a very rich and wonderfully detailed story. The writer can also use certain inner thoughts or plot details to hide or disguise upcoming events, therefore surprising the reader. This should be your challenge goal. As you begin the exploration of the world of writing, strive for using at least the third person point of view, and eventually the third person omniscient point of view as the way in which you think and write. As you become more efficient with using this approach to writing...and thinking about writing, it will become easier. It's actually magical, as the story takes on a life of its own and unfolds right in front of your eyes...and right from your fingertips.

The beginning novelist usually starts with the first person point of view, since the book is usually a story told by one person's point of view. The use of first person pronouns is prevalent in this approach, and it's easier to tell the story with a first person perspective. The challenge is holding the reader's attention for the length of the book, but it can be done. Pat Conroy used the first person point of view in his book, *Beach Music,* as well as *The Water is Wide.* Hemingway, as a contrast, uses third person and third person omniscient. This version of third person, in short, is all knowing. There'll be more in-depth explanation in the following chapters.

The second person point of view is rarely used in writing novels or short stories. It's too bland and doesn't offer the writer any avenues for shifting the conversation or manipulating dialogue to make the story flow.

Many skilled writers may shift from one point of view to another, but this, too, is very tricky. The writer has to remember everything about every character and situation, and to boot, not expose too much of the story plot to the reader. Writing is hard work, and requires constant study and practice from the writer, especially if you're new at this game.

Writing is truly a craft, both an art and a science, that takes years to perfect. Pat Conroy, in his book, *The Reading Life,* spoke of his high school English teacher who taught him not only how the write a good sentence, but also how to read a good sentence. He said that a well written sentence will entice the reader to lust for more. And, so it is.

Chapter 6

Setting and Place

The setting and place of your story is basic and primary to writing. The details of plot and description can add complexity and strength to the construction of your story; however, remember, you are in charge. You are the creator, the orchestra conductor, the coach, etc. Your story can begin as simple and straightforward as describing a *"moonlit night where the silhouettes of the trees danced effortlessly on the glassy surface of the water's edge at famer John's pond."*

Or, you might add something like, *"The icy surface of the lakes in the Upper Peninsula, what is commonly referred to as the UP, hinds itself with winter wind and blowing ice as it freezes time into place."* Stephen Hamilton, who is an ex-cop turned prolific and notable mystery writer, relies heavily and almost exclusively on his past experiences with growing up and working in the UP, the Upper Peninsula of Michigan. Hamilton captures the reader's imagination with his descriptions of time and place, as he unfolds the settings of his stories and the characters they contain. Of course, if you become a follower of any writer who engages the reader in a series of books and stories, you as the reader becomes familiar, even attached to the characters. It's much like the way my mother, God Bless her Soul (as she passed from this world in 2001) would become so enthralled with her soap operas, as they were called, that her descriptions and dialogue about the characters and the twists and turns of the daily and weekly plots would confuse anyone who didn't know that she was talking about her "Soaps!"; whether than describing some cast upon family member who didn't show for the annual family gathering at Thanksgiving three years ago. It can be funny and humorous. In fact, writing about this reference of the imagination of a reader, and in this case, an "on-looker," that being my dear mother, makes me chuckle. But this is exactly what you want to achieve and do as a writer: entice the reader and make the "want" of the story linger.

You need not expect to get your book right the first time. Go to work and revamp or rewrite it. God only exhibits his thunder and lightning at intervals, and so they always command attention. These are God's adjectives. You thunder and lightning too much; the reader ceases to get under the bed, by and by.

- Letter to Orion Clemens, 23 March 1878

Let us guess that whenever we read a sentence & like it, we unconsciously store it away in our model-chamber; & it goes, with the myriad of its fellows, to the building, brick by brick, of the eventual edifice which we call our style.

- Letter to George Bainton, 15 Oct 1888[1]

The act of writing is the creation of the portal to one's heart and soul; the magic of writing is allowing others to peer through it and experience the mystical journey through the caverns of the mind.

The setting and place of your story is yours to create…that is if you are writing fiction. One piece of advice that I will sprinkle all throughout this book, is that you should also guard against revealing anything specific about your book. It would be wise for you to develop a brief description or answer to the general and curious questions you will undoubtedly get when people, family and friends, learn that you are writing a book. Most people will not have the same belief in your dream of writing and publishing a book. But keep focused and keep at it!

****

Setting

The setting of the story is a vitally important element of your writing. It sets the tone, in-part, for the story you are about to unfold, layer by layer, piece by piece.

First printed in The Art of Authorship: Literary Reminiscences, Methods of Work, and Advice to Young Beginners. Personally Contributed by Leading Authors of the Day. Compiled and Edited by George Bainton. New York: D. Appleton and Company, 1890, pp. 85-88.

The setting of a story, or in this case, a book, will set the speed and framework through which the characters in the story, as they are revealed, begin to show the reader their personality and character flaws, which is all part of the tapestry of the story. As the writer, the author of your book, you will weave the plots and subplots together by the use of dialogue and story descriptions. It is through these mechanisms and strategies that the setting is also revealed.

Think about it this way, the setting, time and place of your story will serve as the path from which your narrative will originate and develop. Think about some of Edgar Allan Poe's writings and how he developed stories and tales around mysterious and dark settings. For the avid reader or Poe fan, the beginning of each chapter restarts the clock, one might say, in discovering the clues and solving the mystery.

Consider Agatha Christie's writings and books. Her stories of crime and intrigue were set in a time and place that, at the time, teased the curiosity of every mystery novel reader. Set in earlier times and in London or some other part of England, she weaved parts and portions of the story with twists and turns of plot detail, dialogue between her characters, and various mechanisms of catastrophes, including kidnapping and murder. One of her most famous and notable works, *Murder on the Orient Express*, expanded her plots and subplots to that of a European iconic trip across to the Orient. Wrapped in murder, the elements of greed and jealousy provided the thread for her weaving the mystery. The setting was obviously, a train, but alas, it was much more than an ordinary train. The Orient Express was both a luxury liner as well as a means for "middle class" folks to travel. The fact that its destination was specifically the Orient provided a more narrowly defined group of characters in the story, and later the motion picture. As a writer and creator of stories and novels, you are able to alter the direction, condition, elements, and any part of the setting you wish to change.

Please do not misunderstand me here. The setting and place (and time) are extremely crucial elements to the story you will build within your novel. When developing the idea for your story or novel, you must consider your goals with writing the book. In my view, you should consider your book the next bestseller coming out, even if only your family, friends and/or colleagues purchase a copy. If you have had this burning desire in your head for years to write a novel, then I predict that the fire will be set once you get into the writing and story developing process, and more significantly, when you complete you novel. I remember the inner elation I felt as I was finishing the writing of my first novel. As the story developed (over many years as I toiled off and on), and as I became closer to the latter part of the book, I suddenly realized how the story was going to end.

For my project, I had an original idea that I sketched out on several sheets of stenographer's paper, outlined the first chapter and wrote the first four or five pages of the first chapter. Now, I must say at this point that the beginning of the novel changed drastically, but the original idea remained intact. I labored for years, writing some here and some there, which is something I do not recommend for the serious writer. I have since developed somewhat of a routine when I write, but I'll address this issue later.

Suffice to say when writing a novel, the narrative itself will likely take on a life of its own. Like a runaway train, you may not even see it coming, but it will blast its way through the keyboard as you tap out your story in lightning fashion, and then, you will suddenly realize that the story, your story, has transformed itself into a different and yet surprising outcome. Follow me on this one point. As I was heavily writing my book, and as I was approaching the latter portion of the story, I didn't actually know how it would end. As a writer of an adventure or suspense novel, you have to orchestrate the resolutions and closures within the various sections of the story, all without losing the tease of the reader. For me, as I sat on the screened porch of a 100 year old farm house located on the banks of the Neuse River, near Beaufort, North Carolina, I found myself overtaken by the story itself. It was like the story was controlling my fingers as they pounded the keyboard of my computer. Then, suddenly, with a subtleness that was shocking to my mind, the ending of the story revealed itself. It was like an outer-body experience. All the years and all the sweat and worry and doubt about whether or not I could or would finish writing this book, were suddenly without announcement to the world, coming to a completion. The words rolled through my mind as I crafted the rescue of the characters left in the story, and as they were transported from a foreign country back to the safety and security of the United States. And then the grand finale, the ending of endings, became clear and definitive. Their adventure would end for the moment with the grandest of congratulatory gestures from the highest of all honors, all this aboard the U.S.S. Kerasage, which itself was a symbolic icon associated with my step-father. He served in the Navy during the Korean conflict and was on the U.S.S. Kerasage. Symbolism, place and setting encapsulated this moment. It can encapsulate your story.

At approximately 11:20 P.M., as I sat on the screened porch of that 100 year old farm house that overlooked the Neuse River, and as I typed my closing and last sentence, the elation brought on an emotion rarely felt, that of silent victory, the completion of a difficult journey. I threw my arms in the air and yelled out, "I've finished it; I'm done, finally, I'm done," and as my wife rushed onto the screened porch, I sat back in my chair staring at the computer screen and took a long swig of beer. After hugs and kisses were exchanged, I saved the work again, just to make sure I would not lose it, and then got up and walked around the house and the porch as I was caught up in this strange but elated state. I had just finished my book.

My point is this: I had no idea when I began writing in earnest where or what my setting or place would be. I had no idea, for example, that the primary characters in my novel, *Island Castaways,* would become enthralled in a near coup in a Central American country, and eventually be rescued by an entourage of Navy Seals who were acting under the orders of the Secretary of State and the President of the United States. Writing the ending of the book was not only exciting but exhilarating. The setting and place changed slightly as the story developed, but they were always connected to the storyline and its development.

The following are some helpful hints:

1. Think about what setting, time and place would encapsulate you in a movie theater, and then model your story framework from there.
2. Don't be afraid to be flexible with the setting and place where the plot developments occur.
3. Allow the characters in your story to develop and change, as well as move in and out of the setting, place and time you've set in motion by way of the story.
4. Word of caution: Be mindful of your progression through a timeframe or a number of years. Don't out run the years in the story.
5. Remember, you can always revise and edit your timeframes and slightly alter the setting and place details. When writing, time is an element on your side as an author. Allowing yourself time away from the writing itself will often times provide you clarity as to what adjustments need to be made to make the story more believable and tantalizing.

Chapter 7

Predetermined Outcome vs. Organically Emerging Story

Welcome to the first chapter of your new book...any book. After reading the first chapter of a selected book, can you definitively say what the outcome will be? Perhaps the author is predictable, such as knowing that the main character will survive whatever near-death experience or situation the plots of the book thrusts upon him, but you probably would not know exactly how the details of the story will unfold. This is your clue as to how to think through and write your novel.

There are two approaches with planning how your book will describe the journey of the story. Some people will have a predetermined ending, a place where they, the writer, are aiming for the culmination of all the plots, the twists, the details of the story. A close look at their personal lives may reflect that they, themselves, are very predictable and require a life filled with routines and definitive events.

The other approach described here is that of what I refer to as the organically emerging story. This approach, in my view, is the most complimentary when an author is creating a piece of fiction. Over the past few years, I have reviewed and read about how numerous writers and authors write or create fiction, whether it is a short piece or story or a full-blown novel. In almost every case, the author reflects that she or he relies primarily and almost solely on their ability to summon and discover their muse and inspiration of their creative spirits, and thus, yielding their piece of art, their novel or short story.

Now as I have noted, this approach seems to be completely open-ended and left to a totally evolutionary event. This may work for you personally as a writer; and, it is totally respectable. I recommend, however, that as a writer of fiction, one must employ some level of predictability in the process of creating one's prose. I would also submit that as a writer, one will develop and refine the process of how writing occurs, the planning process of the story or narrative, and will develop a complexity to the writing process that actually forms your personal identity as a writer and author. I believe that this is one, just one, of the reasons why almost all experienced authors will not share or disclose how they write, any part of their drafts except with their editor, and certainly only to full drafts to a select few confidants.

The predetermined approach is useful perhaps in the beginning, if it lends comfort to the writer, knowing that there is an end in mind or target for the story. But don't fall into that trap limitation, in that you become bound by the story in your mind. This is a good practice in the business world, according to Stephen Covey, a noted professional trainer and business consultant whose by-line was to "begin with the end in mind." This approach also fits well with the outline approach I described earlier in this book, much like how we were required to write in high school or college.

In contrast, as a fiction writer, regardless of what genre, one must find the creative genius in their writing, like turning a bunch of hounds loose when hunting for foxes. When they hit the scent of a fox, every part of their being becomes focused on finding the fox. The dog's mind and all its senses come together like the cross between a hand full of sparklers and a box full of M-80s, and the result is pure creative genius.

Another example of what I am attempting to illustrate is related to the following. As a kid growing up in a rural area outside Bessemer, Alabama, in an era where there were three channels on the television and Tom York hosted the Morning Show on WBRC, Channel 6, with a live drawing on a section of his show called Dialing for Dollars, where he used a rotary dial type of phone to place his calls, during the summer months my buddies and I were left to our own creations. One of our creative ideas was to build what we fondly referred to as mud dams…dams like the beavers built. There just happened to be a small creek located near one of my buddy's house and we would scurry down to the creek on occasion to begin our tasks. Writing fiction is much like how we built our mud dams. We knew kind of what we wanted to have at the end of the day, but were open to working on this project for multiple days. Yet, we were kids not of working age. So aside from cutting the grass ("lawn" for you sophisticated readers), we had free-reign of our summer months. We would select our site for the mud dam, and then commence to gathering sticks, rocks or whatever we could find to serve as blockades to the water. Once a sufficient amount of debris and materials had been gathered, we would form a bucket brigade to move our precious materials to the blockade site in the water. We were relentless. Tasks were divided and sequenced as we went. Sometimes different parts of the dam had to be reinforced as progress continued. Eventually we all would be in the creek, up to our knees in water, each one of us feverishly slinging mud, sticks and rocks in their places, constantly looking for leaks or places that needed shoring up, and finally realizing that the water had stopped. The dam was holding. Our task was complete. A momentary silence would fall upon us as we stood in the water, motionless and staring at our creation, and then, without boundaries or muteness, we would jump and scream like little Huck Finn's traveling down the Mississippi. We had done it. We dammed up the creek and the newly formed pond was increasing in volume and width by the minute. Revision of our creation would be necessary.

To me, albeit a recollection from my childhood, this represents the writing of fiction. It reflects life in the details of the plots and twists and outcomes. As a writer, you must discover that out of bounds way of writing, of creating an attention grabbing piece of fiction that makes the reader want to turn the page without realizing how many pages they've just read.

Honestly, this can be accomplished using either approach, the predetermined approach or the organic approach, but I caution you as a new writer to not fall into the traps of limiting factors or the rigidity of an outline. I was very fond of my high school senior English teacher, but the outline approach did not work for me. I was never comfortable with it, even during my college years. I had to find the approach that worked for me. And you must do the same.

Chapter 8

Using Humor & Satire in Writing

Mark Twain is most renowned for utilizing satire and humor in the craft of writing. Today, one can read his stories and become mesmerized with the content and plot twists that are almost always draped with humor or sarcasm but with a twist of southern charm. Even after his demise, he has successfully directed the last orchestration of satiric humor with the directive of not publishing his autobiography before 100 years after his death.

There is an art in using words and language that invoke the reader to express a grin or to laugh aloud, or even to snicker a little. I suppose that this sill can be taught, but more likely I suspect it must be developed internally from the person, through countless readings of good literature and the study of satire and humor. A deliberate act of attempting to insert a humoristic flare to one's writing would be like trying to shooting a bow and arrow without ever having had instruction or study as to how to do it. The arrow most likely would go sailing away from the target, or at the very least, connect with the extreme edge of the target. Much study and practice is required in order to master the fine art of humor and satire in writing, but do not hesitate to try it. In the world of a writer, using humor and satire is like going skinny dipping as a teenager. Only your closest friends will know and they'll be sworn to secrecy, but all of you will stand nervously on the sidelines after your book is published and listen for the reactions to the strategically placed words and phrases, listening for the quiet snicker or that sudden gasp that occurs unexpectedly just before a person catches themselves from laughing out loud.

Listen to your conversations with people as well, especially those closest to you. Listen for the laughter. What caused it? Who said what to whom and in what context and setting? Once you figure that out, replicate it. The secret to Ernest Hemingway's writing success and the reason he is credited with changing the literary world, is that he used short declarative sentences and used dialogue to carry his stories forward to each end. Aside from the fact that he was also a charter member, as it were, of a literary renaissance of those who identified themselves as ex-patriots, and thus traveled abroad in search of inspiration for his writing, Hemingway used his life experiences as backdrops as well as front stage props for his stories. Hemingway was always in search of happiness. He was restless. He was ruthless with his writing, easily angered by criticism, and his sarcasm often times provided the backdrop for his twists and plotlines. In his younger days, Hemingway was egotistical and self-absorbed and admitted such, which also became a source for his satire and humor.

Another source that I highly recommend is that of Southern genre writers. There is an organization of southern writers and they have a yearly conference at various locations in, of course, the South. But if you want to study how humor and satire are used in writing, in the rawest of forms, read some of the little known southern authors. One book that comes to mind as I write this chapter is entitled, *A Sweet Jug of Tea: Southern Short Stories,* by Mike Zealy, published in 2012. As one who hails from Alabama, as do I, he recounts his loves, his hates, and life experiences as a southern boy whose mindset and attitudes ran incongruent with his beloved homeland inasmuch as he left the South in search of truth and contentment only to return years later as an adult and after living in New York for a number of years. The stories and places he recounts are lined with sarcastic humor, which frankly makes for interesting reading.

Another author I recommend for readership and study of style, satire and humor is Elmore Leonard. Frankly, pick any of his books. Read them. Read them for the story and pleasure of reading, but also read them for studying style and content. His books are entertaining and stand as iconic examples of good writing from the pioneer era when writers came from obscure places and with a wide variety of motivations for their writings. Such an author and writer was Elmore Leonard. Like many other writers who appeared from out of nowhere, Elmore Leonard was an insurance salesman by day and a late night, cigarette-smoking writer by night. He produced short novels containing stories that engrossed readers who could find themselves in and out before dawn ready for the next book, all without realizing how quickly Elmore Leonard's stories would move them along the highways of time. This made them want even more, and Elmore Leonard provided them with as much and as many as they could read.

As a kid in the sixth grade and on up through high school, I was introduced to the short western stories written by Louis L'amour. The stories were somewhat risqué for the time, and certainly so for a young school lad as myself. My buddy from across the way (through the woods behind the church which was directly across the road from my house, and where my buddy and I both attended) and I had to sneak around to read the scandalous westerns that were filled with horse chases, gunfights, bar room brawls, implied sexual scenes both consensual and explicit descriptions of those that were results of attacks on settlers or travelers going out west. But we didn't read his books for the sexual scenes, as we were embarrassed frankly. Besides, the sermons we were subjected to by the infamous and giant of a man, Brother Melvin Coleman, as we called him, were like the Raid insect commercials, seeking out and exposing even the slightest of our brush with "sinful ways." Somehow, the Reverend would know that we had been up to no-good, and would launch his seek and destroy missiles of repent now or be doomed for hell on a fast train south, such that I'm guessing that we both looked like two cats who had just snagged the canaries. Yet, we never confessed our sins of reading Louis L'amour's adventurous and sometimes scandalous westerns. We just kept reading. The thing I recall most, as a point here, is that those stories, although a little on the edge for a young teenage boy who led a pretty much sheltered life, was like a motion picture in my mind. It provided for me the images of the Wild West, of horses and saloons and cattle drives. They were entrancing and with each story, the characters and plot twists drew you as the reader into the scene as if you were overlooking the shootout from behind a boulder on the hill overlooking the stagecoach transfer station. You could taste the dust in your mouth as if you were in the stage coach when it was stopped and robbed at gunpoint on the way to its destination. L'amour's stories were tantalizing and left the reader wanting more.

My recommendation is that you find authors and writers who are both well-known and those who are not-so-well-known. Read them for the enjoyment as well as for style and content. Then try your hand at writing a short story using your newfound styles of humor and satire.

Chapter 9

The Art and Science of Writing Consistently

As you make your way through the mountains and valleys of writing, on the way to becoming an author of whatever degree, you will no doubt be faced with the issue of writing consistently. It is both an art and a science. And, yes, it can be conquered! Read on.

The first thing you need to know about becoming a successful writer is that you have to write every day - every morning, noon or evening, or at some point during your day, you as a person on the journey of becoming an author must perform this act of writing. There is something magical to writing. It's like entering a world that you control without realizing the fullness of your power. It doesn't matter how well you write, just write. (This is another one of my declarations about my view of writing that will probably send shockwaves throughout the halls of traditionalists, like my beloved senior English teacher, Mrs. Reed.) If you want to complete your novel or writing project within the timeframe you've set, then you have to write consistently, and that means everyday if at all possible.

The amount of pages, words, or time that you write can provide the markers or parameters needed to set yourself in motion for writing. Writing a certain number of pages or words, or writing for a predetermined amount of time will guide you, but do not hesitate to go beyond these mail markers if you find yourself on a roll. Just go with it. Walter Mosley, in his book, *This Year You Write Your Novel* (2007), said that there "are two reasons for this rule – the time you decide on is also the time when you will do your best work – getting the work done and connecting with your unconscious mind" (p. 7).

The goal should be, and by some must be, to write consistently every day. The discipline and nuances derived from writing every day and for establishing these routines will aid in your development as a writer, as well as unlock your subconscious from which all of your writing ideas will emerge. But if you set your routine and suddenly find yourself devoid of ideas or sentences to write or produce, don't panic. This is a common and somewhat normal occurrence. Stephen King writes about this very thing in his book, *On Writing,* where he declares, as does Mosley, that this is the reality of being a writer. Allow yourself time to mentally develop and nurture the ideas and details of your writing that are first born within and then reproduced on paper.

Once you make the switch in your mind to thinking of yourself as a writer, your eyes become the windows for your mind for collecting ideas and thoughts for developing stories, plot lines and plot twists, and all other elements of the story. Even having dinner with your spouse or friends in a restaurant will place you in a position of observation and absorbance. You will hear or observe conversations and interactions between people and will immediately make mental notes for future reference to some part of a story or plot sequence that is orbiting in your mind.

As a writer, you must "loosen the bonds" (Mosley, 2007) of social and familial connections in order for the conscious and subconscious mind to engage itself in moments of creativity, thus producing some form of narrative that invokes the allure of readership. Along with these ball and chains of modern social and mental development comes the fear of failure and of criticism. The successful writer must protect him or herself from these medieval twins whose only purpose is to rip and destroy all who strive to achieve some task or milestone that is noteworthy and that has within its lineage a connection to prominence and circumstance. In other words, write without fear and dread. As my dissertation advisor told me during the five year process of devising and completing doctoral research in the field of educational leadership, "You are the expert in your research." One day during the latter half of my fifth year, as time was drawing near and the deadlines were looming, I came to a realization. It was my "aha" moment. I was indeed the expert of my research. The body or written work was as editorially correct as it could have been. Every word on every page had passed through the university's recommended and strongly suggested editors and had met the rigorous requirements for mechanics and format. The content and findings of the research belonged to me. The interviews had been long completed and transcribed. The archival data had been gathered, categorized and applied within the template of methodology of the research model. The findings had been deduced and described. The written work was done. All that was left to complete was a final defense and submissions of final copies to the Dean's office. On this day, the day I realized that I was indeed the expert on my research, I declared that my work on the written portion of this long journey was completed. Simply, I took charge of my journey and pushed the process across the finish line, and graduated. You, too, must take charge of your writing and the writing project goals, whether it is a book, a short story, or a chapter. Set your routine and engage the discipline of writing, and do it with the utmost confidence and positive energy and outlook. Expect that you will write a great piece of narrative.

As Walter Mosley said, "Don't let any feeling keep you from writing. Don't let the world slow you down. Your story is the most important thing coming down the line this year. It's your year---make the most of it" (p.13).

So, get started.

Chapter 10

The Art of Southern Dialect & Dialogue

Southern Dialect and Dialogue
By Candice W. N. Lawrence

Many writers will unashamedly admit that dialogue can be one of the most difficult elements of storytelling. One has to make the dialogue sound realistic, make it sound believable, make it comprehensible, make it move the story forward, and make it interesting. There are several ways to accomplish this. But the way that works best for me is simple: don't overthink it.

Listen to how people talk in everyday conversation. Sometimes they break up their thoughts. Sometimes they edit their thoughts, revealing only bits and pieces of information, but the intended listeners still understand the context because of their relationship with the speaker. People don't always say exactly what needs to be said, either. For example, if you're talking with your friends about something that happened earlier today at work, chances are, you will not need to say where you were or what your occupation is to get the story out. Plus, depending on your friendship, some details are simply implied or understood. Your friend probably already knows that you are a cat person so you won't have to verbally explain that while telling them about your neighbor's dog keeping you up all night. The more you pay attention to the way people speak, the faster you will develop an ear for dialogue. Eventually you'll grow to "hear" the way people or characters speak and you'll know exactly what they would or would not say. At this point, dialogue will become second nature.

Let's look at some examples of dialogue. In this scenario, we'll have two speakers who are very familiar with one another, around the same age, and have the same circle of friends.

"Matthew called," I told her.

"What'd he want?"

"Rachel's number."

"Isn't she still with Luke?"

"Yeah, I told him. I gave him Annie's number instead."

"It's about time someone got them together. She's liked him since sixth grade," said Alice.

Now let's look at the same scenario, but fill in every possible blank with the implied information.

"Matthew, the guy from our organic chemistry class who dresses in suits every day, called me this afternoon," I told her.

"What was he calling you for?"

"He wanted me to give him my cousin Rachel's phone number so that he could ask her out on a date."

"Oh, okay, is Rachel still dating Luke? Did you tell Matthew that Rachel is with Luke?"

"Yes, Rachel is still dating Luke and I told Matthew that she is Luke's girlfriend. I decided to hook Matthew up with Annie, so I gave him her phone number so that he can ask her out instead."

"That's a great idea. Annie has liked Matthew since we were all in the sixth grade together at Bloomingdale-Chatham Academy. Annie will be so happy to finally get together with him."

Notice this second example is not as believable because the two speakers have known Matthew at least since the sixth grade, yet they identify him as the guy from their college organic chemistry course instead of someone they've known since they were eleven or twelve. Furthermore, there is a lot of unneeded information stated in the second example, such as the name of the school. And there is also some unnecessary repetition. This is an example of where the dialogue gets too over the top and it slows down the scene. Plus, no one really talks like this—especially friends who are in their twenties and who have grown up together. This is why it's important to know your fictional characters—and for them to know each other. Now, the first example conveys the same necessary information so that we immediately understand the relationships between the speakers and the other characters mentioned. It also speeds up the pace, creates a consistent, quick rhythm, and keeps the reader interested. Another thing to remember with dialogue is that you have more leeway as far as grammar and usage or mechanics.

For dialogue, you can omit certain words here and there as long as it does not alter the sentence meaning. However, this is more advanced and should only be done after one has developed an ear for dialogue.

On that note, for those of us interested in southern characters, we often want our characters to be as authentic as possible. For many, this includes dialect. Dialect isn't just regional; it can depend on social class, education, or even pure emphatic usage. Being from Georgia, I've also noticed that two people originally from the same city may have completely different dialects and some people switch their dialect on and off like a tap. There are also cases when depending on context, a speaker will say something with a southern accent, then five minutes later say the same thing but change the pronunciation. Take the word "aunt." I've heard it pronounced as both "ant" and "ain't" by the same person. The only difference was a subconscious decision to shift depending on if the speaker was talking *to* the aunt or *about* the aunt.

I have been taught that dialect should always be consistent throughout a piece of work; however, my personal experiences have shown me that people don't always speak that way. Sometimes they change the stressed syllables, and sometimes they omit letters or syllables. Still some things are easier to interpret and understand orally as opposed to on paper. This being said, try to aim for a happy medium between consistent and authentic. If your character tends to say something one way and then change it a few minutes later, be consistent with that. If your character's dialect is the same in any given conversation, be consistent with that as well.

Again, before writing a character's dialect, develop an ear for the dialects used in the characters region or area. This can take some time, but it will always be worth it. If possible, talk with a wide range of people in the intended setting: young, old, area natives, those who have only lived there for a few years, etc. This will help you develop an idea of what your character(s) would really sound like in that region. It will also help you understand what factors cause him or her to speak the way he or she does. Remember, when overthought, dialogue—and dialect for that matter—can be dangerous territory, but with the right research and a keenly developed ear, you'll be mastering the techniques in no time.

Chapter 11

Finding Inspiration

By Candice W. N. Lawrence

The best thing about inspiration is that it's for you and you alone. The quote, picture, song, person, situation that inspires your work is simply that: the thing that inspires *you* to write. There are no rights or wrongs when it comes to inspiration (...just try to keep it legal and ethical). Finding inspiration is probably the freest part of the writing process and that applies for any type of writing. The thing that inspires you may be something you choose to keep private, or intimate, or it may even appear in your story.

The act of *finding* inspiration involves an almost trancelike state of openness called daydreaming. It happens where your mind teeters between *what if* and *what next*. It often occurs while cooking, reading, driving (or riding), listening to music or a speech, looking at an image, showering, exercising, and yes, it can even happen while one is literally dreaming. Basically, it can happen anytime you allow your mind to wonder about the story behind the thing(s) captivating you. That's where you find yourself imagining characters, storylines, settings, and plots.

Inspiration can be as simple as seeing an image on a notebook and coming up with characters who live in the image's setting; it can also be as simple as listening to two strangers talking, then jotting down how you think the rest of the conversation or situation would play out.

When you're intentionally or actively seeking out inspiration, think of it as a spy mission. You don't want to cause too much self-intrusion; you just want to get the information you need then discreetly get out of there. Blend in, but keep in mind the words of J.K. Rowling's Mad Eye Moody, "Constant vigilance!"

Try doing any of the following missions:

- Sit in a semi-crowded restaurant and pay attention to the surroundings such as wardrobe, body language, conversations. Now think of reasons why the people may be there. Could they be celebrating a birthday or reuniting after five years in different states? Jot down some notes about the story behind them dinning out.

- Sit in a park. Take time to notice the various types of people and their activities. Are people running in groups or couples or individually? Does one person seem more focused or more lethargic? Could the runners be training for that marathon that's been on their bucket list since childhood? Could the runners be trying to condition themselves to join the Army? Write a few brief notes about the small things that catch your attention.

NOTE: *You may also want to consider visiting these places at different days and/or times as this will gather different types of crowds. For example, going to a restaurant around the lunch hour may bring in business executives and going on a Friday or Saturday night will recruit more of a diverse crowd. Basically, different crowds produce different atmospheres, leading to a multitude of ideas.*

- Arrive a little earlier to class or a meeting one day. Watch your fellow students or co-workers as they file in. Do any of them seem unreasonably chipper? Does anyone enter with 0.324 seconds left to spare? Focus on facial expressions and in some cases wardrobe (only if there is something unique there—remember, we're staying on the legal and ethical side of things). For example, did the late classmate arrive in a Cracker Barrel uniform? If so, maybe he has to dash from work on certain days to get to class. Think about why he may be working there and unravel your story from there. If you're not in college yet, watch your classmates' faces as homework is being collected. Does anyone seem anxious or excited? Quickly scribble a list of reasons why he or she didn't have his or her homework.

  Once you get home, review the notes you've taken. Is there anything you find yourself curious about?

Start writing about it. You may find ways to intertwine some of the elements from the restaurant with the park. For example, was one of the diner customers the fiancé of the man conditioning himself in the park? If so, think about why they may be in different places and the challenges they face in their future.

You may want to compile your notes into a file or folder. Even if you do not use everything, hang on to it! It might come in handy for another story later. Soon you will see that you have ample material for multiple stories, characters, and plots. When you find yourself hitting a dead end, open files or folders and see which of those fresh ideas you can incorporate into your story.

NOTE: *Be sure to make a note of which ideas, quotes, and characters you have used so that they don't accidently reappear in another story.*

If you're lucky, sometimes inspiration creeps up on *you*. When you are stuck in traffic, doing homework, or preparing that report your boss assigned to you and you hear a first line or a small segment of dialogue between two unfamiliar characters or an unfamiliar setting, know that inspiration is knocking. Listen up!

When all else fails, put your spy gear on (a handy notepad and pen or pencil will suffice—or you can go high-tech) and keep your eyes open and hears listening at all times.

Chapter 12

Circles of Support and Encouragement

By: Candice W. N. Lawrence

When I graduated from high school and during my college years, the most common question directed at me was also my most dreaded question: "What are you going to do/be?" After expressing that I wanted to be an author, I was usually slapped with enough doubting comments and scrutinizing questions that at times, I just wanted to say, "teach" instead of "write" just to avoid the negativity (such as "You won't make any money," or "What are you really going to do?") stemming from the questioner. Each time most of these conversations ended with me frustrated, angry, and a little more determined to share my stories. It's amazing how many people will write off someone else's writing career before ever hearing or reading a single paragraph of the person's work. With as much outward negativity there is, you must have just as much, if not more, belief in your story. Furthermore, you have to have a tightknit circle of support and continuous encouragement. It's not necessary for each member of your circle to know each other, just make sure you have a close, trustworthy relationship with each member.

I cannot reiterate this point enough to new writers. It's crucial to have trust. From that trust stems genuine support and encouragement. Often, people will appear interested in your projects initially, or in small talk, but your close circle should be the bulk of your support and encouragement. These are the people from whom you never doubt their sincerity. These are the people who will help you decide when it's time to divorce an idea, or who will continue to motivate you, or offer a perspective of your writing through an undiscovered lens. These are often the people who are your first readers and your strongest advocates.

I have had countless in-depth conversations with my brother in regards to encouragement. Out of the two of us, Jonathan was the big reader when we were growing up. Still, he never expressed any doubt towards my sudden interest in reading and writing during my high school years. To this day, we have hour long talks in which he spends time encouraging me to continue writing; after each conversation, I feel refreshed and motivated. Likewise, it's also nice to have my parents believe in and uplift me. While I may not go into extensive detail about my writing projects with my family, it's an immeasurable amount of encouragement to have such unshakable support.

Throughout the years, I have also gained support from some of the most unexpected sources, including one of my favorite professors whom supported me before she and I ever officially met. Once Dr. George and I finally met (we heard about each other via Columbus State University's English Department), she would take the time to talk with me about my writing, as well as different reading and publication opportunities I should try. She and some of my other former professors continue to be tremendous sources of encouragement for me.

I have found that having book-loving friends with similar literary tastes as your own (or who enjoy writing that is similar to your writing style) brings in assurance and excitement to your own work. For one, it's reassuring to know you are not the only person who likes to read a certain genre or author, and it's also motivating to read and discuss authors who inspire you. Often these friendships lead to loads of book recommendations for authors and techniques you may want to study while honing your own craft. One of the sweetest things about this is being able to discuss these books without any fear of scolding or judgment from your friends. A best friend of mine, Liz Lockhart, often shares great titles with me. Thanks to her, I began reading Jasper Fforde's Thursday Next series, which incorporates many of my own interests while offering ample writing techniques and devices—such as literary puns, successfully incorporating references to classics like *Jane Eyre*, and unpredictable plot twists—that I admire and want to master. Liz is also a great writer herself, so it's nice to be able to send her drafts or throw her ideas to get her honest, useful feedback and encouragement.

On that note, it's also beneficial to have friends who are working on their own stories, that way you all can bring your pieces together and critique them. I was involved in a group like this at CSU. A couple of classmates and I decided to have a roundtable at least once a week, bringing in whatever individual writing project we were working on, to receive suggestions and get a new perspective on our work that had previously been un-work shopped or read by anyone else. These meetings also showed us what was working, or provoking the intended reader reaction, and what was unclear and unintentionally likely to be misconstrued. For those who struggle with writing routines and would like a little added accountability, these small groups work great and typically benefit all participants equally.

Another unexpected source of support and encouragement can arise from relationships between previously published authors and writers who are eager to be published. I have met and spoken with numerous published authors—talk about humbling, intimidating, and inspiring experiences—and most welcome the chance to chat with other writers, when their schedules permit it. Often these authors share encouragement during conversations. Keep in mind that published authors may not always be accessible, however, you'd be surprised at how many respond to letters or emails. Even if you only meet the author once, his words will continue to be an inspirational boost.

There are many ways you can build your circle of support and encouragement, and these are just a few examples to get started creating or expanding your own group. I have a growing circle of people I consider trustworthy and genuine, ranging from my brother and parents to close friends, professionals, and mentors. Make sure you carefully establish your group, and consider having a diverse group. Not all encouragers have to be writers. Remember, not every person who reads your published work will have a background in writing. It also does not hurt to have people of different ages and experiences supporting you along the way. After all, your circle is there to lift you up when the negativity gets too suffocating and to help you remember why you write in the first place: it's your passion.

Chapter 13

Developing the Plot

So you have this idea for a book. You even have the idea for scenes and characters and perhaps some degree of story-line, but what about the actual plot? How many plot twists and turns and layers will your story have? How will you weave each layer and twist them together in unassuming ways in order to eventually bring your story to an unexpected end? These are the questions that should at least start your planning and writing process. With writing this chapter on plot development, I will also assume that you have gotten past the nah-sayers and doubting Thomas's and have set yourself with great expectations.

The plot of the story is akin to the seeds one plants in a garden with only the gardener knowing what has been planted. The garden becomes mystic when people try to figure and contemplate what has been planted and why. As the sprigs begin to break the surface of the dirt, a flurry of activity erupts when the word spreads like wildfire about the garden coming to life. "What has the gardener planted?" One may ask. And all along, the gardener has been providing little information about the mystery of seeds he has planted. He has refused to reveal from where he purchased or traded for the seeds. So much so that some locals began a search one farming coop store at a time, asking if the gardener had been there, had he purchased or traded for seeds and if so, what?

****

Were you captured by the aforementioned paragraphs about the gardener and the mystery behind the seeds? As you read it, did you find yourself wanting to know what all the fuss was about? And did the short depiction of a gardener with unidentified seeds reveal anything about the plot directly, or did it draw in the reader? Exactly!

My first recommendation for a newly proclaimed writer, and particularly if this is your first novel, become a student of plot development in fiction and short stories. Read some particularly well acclaimed stories and books. Read such authors as Elmore Leonard (whom I've mentioned before), Stuart Woods, Agatha Christie, Steve Hamilton (who writes mystery and whodunit stories set in the UP, Upper Peninsula of northern Michigan), or Syd Fields who became known as the Father of Screenplays. Why screenplays you might ask? First, read the book, and you'll find the answers to your questions. But, in short, think about screenplays or movies. A great movie will transport you in a timeless fashion to the very setting of the movie. The sights and sounds of every scene take over your very mind and imagination, and even physiologically alter your breathing, your heartbeats, and your emotions. And when the movie is over, it takes a minute for your senses to return to normal. This is what you should strive for with your story, whether it's a short story or a full length book.

In his book, *Four Screenplays: Studies in the American Screenplay*, the late great Syd Field wrote, "Screenwriting is a craft that occasionally rises to the level of art. Like film, it is a unique and special form that is constantly shifting and changing, mirroring the needs and concerns of our time. As a result, each generation brings a new eye and a new sensibility to the screenplay (p. 19)." This statement by Syd Field can be applied to the craft of authorship. For the screenplay and motion picture alike, books, novels, and short stories have a similar path of existence. There is an established standard of mechanics, structure and methodology for writing a successful story or novel. There are critics who will spill your blood and theirs as they slice and dice your book. Then, there's the readership, the individual reader who perhaps latches onto you as a writer, reads everything you produce and publish. Some readers only care about the entertainment value of your story, your plot twists, and the moment when the movie of the mind is over. Your story can even be predictable and some readers will have nothing but praise and will continue to purchase your books. Take Stuart Woods as an example. To date, he has written approximately 27 books featuring a lead character named Stone Barrington. Thus far, although sometimes dicey, the reader can figure that Mr. Barrington will emerge from each plot twist and near misses of his demise at the end of the book, back in his office with a Knob Creek in hand. The character of Stone Barrington has become iconic, something of a modern day James Bond of New York, complete with his own source of gadgetry.

As the plot or plots reveal themselves, they must become the super train that transports the reader throughout the story. Aside from short declarative sentences and dialogue, Hemingway also used settings and events from around the world as backdrops of his novels and short stories. The settings and places also provided Hemingway with story and plot details in which he could insert in order to peak the reader's curiosity, keeping the reader engaged in the story. His book, *Islands in the Stream,* which was published posthumously, was to be Hemingway's newest great novel. It was actually a compilation of three novelettes that moved the same characters through a period of many years, a war, and post-war events. The book, *The Mystery of Edwin Drood,* by Charles Dickens, was both full of mysterious plot twists and turns, but also was a mystery itself. The book was unfinished when Charles Dickens died, and according to his will, he provided instructions for how the novel was to be finished and by whom. At the time, around 1915, it was said that the penmanship was directed by the ghost and influence of Charles Dickins's spirit. It was remarked that the writing was true to form with its "austerity and simplistic style;" however, the book was filled with mystery, of unexpected turns and plot twists.

As you begin your writing, build the walls that protect and hide the coming ending of the story. Perhaps this is why Margaret Mitchell, while writing her only novel, *Gone with the Wind,* began with the last chapter and wrote the story from the last chapter to the beginning. Albeit a strange and unusual approach, the story and book is hailed as a significant piece of writing for the times.

As we have discussed the aspects of plot development, it reminds me why I personally do not like the traditional outline method associated with the planning process of writing. For me, it's too limiting and does not provide that visual one might need to develop effective and surprising plot-lines.

So, how does a writer build and construct the plot?

It begins with the first paragraph of page one of the first chapter. It has been suggested that a good writer will have the reader hooked and left wanting more after the first five pages. If you are writing a piece of creative fiction, I will remind you now that you are the creator of this piece of art, this story, thus, you are the expert and mastermind behind the story.

In the first pages, create your catastrophe and hook within those five pages, but don't reveal your main story line. Keep it hidden as long as you can. Another example of good plot development is that of radio entertainment programs. One in particular is Garrison Keillor's Prairie Home Companion, which features stories and skits with unusual characters and stories. The show itself is a "throw-back" to the Radio Days when there was no television. One of the show's main pieces is "The News from Lake Wobegone," set in rural Minnesota and features a cast of characters with plot twists that are totally local and soap opera-ish, but can be quite funny and entertaining. I listen to the show often as I am driving from my residence in Savannah to Charleston (to visit with my granddaughters) or Atlanta (to visit with my grandson), and it's very entertaining. My wife and I even saw the radio show many years ago at the Johnny Mercer Theater in Savannah, long before we moved here. But my point simply is that writing requires your imagination. Just like in the radio shows, one has to use their imagination to create the scenes in their mind. The same thought applies to writing, especially writing with a plot filled with mystery and intrigue...and maybe a dead body.

Chapter 14

Characters: Protagonist, Antagonist, Supporting

By: Candice W. N. Lawrence

Think of your best friend or a group of your closest friends. You know them well. You know their whole name, favorite color, favorite band, birthday, hometown; you also know the deeper things that make them uniquely themselves. Maybe they're from a military family so they aren't really used to staying in one place long, which can sometimes make them seem apathetic towards branching out to new relationships. Maybe they grew up volunteering with their family in church, so getting their hands and knees dirty with community service is an enriching, habitual commitment for them. While these things may not be mentioned regularly or upon first being introduced, they are all important facts to understanding 1) why your friends are the way that they are and 2) how to respond, relate, and interpret them.

With that said, regard your characters as you would your closest friends. Take time to not only familiarize yourself with the characters, but also get to know them on a personal level, outside the realm of the plot you're working on. Make a playlist for them, find out their hobbies, fears, important dates or events in their lives, their origins (don't stop at just that one character, think about their parents, grandparents, siblings, etc.). Discover what makes them, them. Furthermore, let your characters reveal these traits to you instead of forcing them into a specific mold. If this seems difficult, try slipping into character. How would he or she react in a certain situation? Why?

Learn their back-story or background to figure out why they say and do certain things. Often, characters display quirky traits that can be pivotal in a story, such as one character's dialect leading a major character to misunderstand geographical directions; or a character can't bring himself to understand the concept of loyalty because in the past, he has never had someone to be loyal to and vice versa. On the other hand, some quirks may not greatly impact the story's plot, but they are still interesting to make note of. For example, your main character may have the same birthday as her grandmother; it may not be significant to the storyline and it may not even make it to the final draft, but it's still an interesting tidbit and it goes to show that you've taken the time to thoroughly develop, know, and understand your character.

Now that we know our characters, let's determine their worth. This is actually kind of like a trick question. Like people, all characters are important in that they play a role in the larger scheme of things. This is another reason why it's important to learn the backstories of every character. Sometimes the seemingly "irrelevant" character causes a small action which triggers several larger events (cue the plot twists!). Still, it is important to have a clear understanding of who the protagonist (the good guy), the antagonist (the bad guy), and the supporting characters are.

Protagonists are usually the characters that the storyline centers around. Generally, the protagonist desires something or needs to accomplish something but there is an obstacle or conflict—albeit person (internal or external), nature, or object—blocking his or her way. More often than not, the protagonist is the guy—or gal—readers are rooting for. When writing as the protagonists, keep in mind that there should be a level of connection, attachment, or relatable feelings between the reader and the character. This doesn't mean change who the character is to fit your audience; it merely means that it should be clear to the reader why the protagonist acts, thinks, or talks the way she does. Often, the storyline follows the protagonist's pursuit in attaining or accomplishing a desired outcome.

As the overgrown—internal or external—mutant standing in the way of the protagonist's goals, we have the antagonist or villain. These guys and gals are the reason why there is a story, in that they generate the tension within the plot. Without them, the protagonist would already have what he or she is after—thus, eliminating the need to write the story. Antagonists come in several forms. They can be internal, such as the protagonist's fear to face a large crowd; they can also be external, such as the monster in our closets or under our beds that we've all run away from, or Lex Luthor, Superman's nemesis. As for external antagonists, some writers feel that there should always be a reason why the villain is bad. For example, he may have grown up in poverty and decided to turn to crime as a means of survival or she may have suffered a traumatizing event or illness which causes her to inflict pain on others such as Charlotte Brontë's menacing character Bertha Rochester in *Jane Eyre*. On the other hand, some of the vilest antagonists are the ruthless ones who commit evil acts just for the sake of being evil, such as Jasper Fforde's antagonist Acheron Hades in *The Eyre Affair*. It's up to you (and to some extent, your villain) to determine how evil your antagonist should be and if his or her motives are justifiable or not.

NOTE: *Justifiable motives can lead to readers understanding and somewhat sympathizing with the antagonist, causing the reader to feel slightly torn between the protagonist and antagonist. Unjustifiable motives, like being evil for the thrill of it, will often cause readers to feel even more anger, frustration, or hatred towards the antagonist.*

Last but certainly not least are our supporting characters. Even though these are sometimes called "flat characters" (protagonists and antagonists are "round"), they can still have important effects. These characters range from offering comedic relief to accidently setting off a spiral of events for the main characters. In other words, they can help slow down the plot or quicken it despite not being central to the storyline. When writing about supporting characters, give them a backstory, too. You'd be surprised how many supporting characters end up as main characters because of discoveries found in developmental backstories.

In a nutshell, despite of the role he or she plays (protagonist, antagonist, or supporting), find out why the character plays the part the way he or she does and how it affects the storyline and surrounding characters.

Chapter 15

Believe in Your Story: It's Your Creation
and You're the Expert
By Candice W. N. Lawrence

Ask any new writer what his or her occupation is and you'll hear one of two answers: 1) an enthusiastic "I'm a writer" or 2) a mousy "I want to be a writer." Both phrases express interest in a career in writing; however, there is a difference between the two. Assuming that the person has already started writing, the difference in *wanting to be* and *am* is simply, confidence.

Sylvia Plath wisely explained, "The worst enemy of creativity is self-doubt." The moment you begin doubting your writing, is the precise moment your story crumbles. There is a level of confidence that you must have in your work. This confidence, never to be confused with arrogance, should be present throughout all stages of your writing process and it should remain even after your books are on shelves. It stems from knowing your story. You have spent the time and effort to skillfully develop each character as well as the setting and plot. You know your story better than anyone else does; therefore, you have the right to wholeheartedly believe in it.

Believing in your work entails being able to discuss or develop elements of your work without doubt or uncertainty. It entails self-respect for the effort you have put forth into making your story come to life. Believing in your story ranges from having a high regard for your creation to trusting that you have portrayed your fiction in the most believable way for your readers.

Furthermore, in the fiction realm, we have a thing called "suspension of belief." This means that for the purposes of following along with fictional work, readers temporarily dispel "that can't happen" notions and replace them with sheer belief that anything can happen (because it *is* fiction, after all). On the other hand, we do have to make sure elements make sense in order to help readers more easily believe in our stories. For example, we wouldn't have a protagonist randomly sprout wings because he needs to travel across town to make an important business meeting; instead, we would either incorporate flight earlier in the story or leave that element out completely—especially since the mode of transportation is not pivotal to the plot.

That said, it is crucial to remember that you are the expert as far as content (characterization, setting, plot, etc.) goes—which is why you will need to know all aspects of your story, in case you are bombarded with interested readers' questions. Readers realize that the story is *yours* to tell. You have the answers because you have immersed yourself in your fictional world on a level deeper than what even the most avid readers can imagine. No matter how much one studies your work, you will always know a little more about the story because of the developmental exploration you conducted while first learning or creating your characters and plotlines. (And because, as of yet, no human can look directly inside your imagination—although the detailed writer has ways of treating readers with vivid glimpses.)

As Mignon McLaughlin stated, "A critic [or reader] can only review the book he has read, not the one which the writer wrote." This is not to say ignore everything every critic or editor says about your work. It merely reminds us that we are the creators and experts of our material and since the bulk of the fiction derives from our imaginations, we have a little more insight on matters such as the tone of voice a character has or what type of attire she wears and why she really ends up turning down that proposal in chapter 27.

If you find yourself feeling uncertain about your story, try reading some of your notes or deleted scenes or returning to what originally sparked your idea for the storyline. Remember that inspiration you found. This will help boost your excitement about the work which in turn will restore that necessary confidence. The more you know about your own work, the more exciting it will become, the more exciting your work is, the more you will believe in your work.

Chapter 16

Celebrate your writing goals!

As I sit down to begin this chapter, I am reminded of how the writing process for me evolves. I have to assume that you as the reader have gathered some motivation and determination toward beginning or completing your writing project. Celebrating your writing is essential. As you set goals or markers for your writing, whether it's a chapter a weekend or a daily pace of producing a set amount of pages or words, celebrating your accomplishments as a writer takes on a significance that can provide reassurance during times when you need it the most.

Celebrating your writing goals, what does this mean exactly? It is up to you, the author of your project, to define what and when you will celebrate. My suggestion, especially starting out, is to set short goals, like completing a chapter. The life as a writer, especially a fiction novelist, is defined by the characters and story lines that come from the imagination. For example, one might find himself suddenly inspired by something they see or hear driving down the road or riding a train. In my view, finding inspiration (See the chapter on Inspiration) is closely connected with celebrating goals. As a fiction writer, you have to set your mind free from the constraints of your daily life, in order to see and hear those small but significant hints for ideas of a story, a plot, characters and other parts of your writing project.

Even as a non-fiction writer, one has to be focused and possess a strong sense of intention in order to complete the task of writing. Some will say that being an author or a writer is sometimes a lonely vocation. And perhaps for some it is; however, I would submit that the vocation as a writer or author is akin to being a builder or a train engineer, any other role or job where one has to utilize their imagination, their intuition and training.

While working on my doctoral research at Vanderbilt, I had a professor by the name of Terry Deal, whose passion was the culture of schools and organizations. It was an invaluable experience having Terry Deal as one of my major professors, and who also eventually served on my dissertation committee. Through his classes, he emphasized the importance of celebration. In schools and organizations, it is important to celebrate the goals and milestones. The act of celebrating provides the glue that builds the bonds of connection and synergy for those who are a part of the school or organization. So, celebration is important. As a writer and author, you are the expert on your story and topic. Celebration, therefore, should be a part of what you do as a writer.

Brain Lamb has a show called "Q&A" for over 20 years on C-Span as well as a show called "Booknotes." On both of these shows, he interviews noted authors and reviews their new books. For me, it's a fascinating show because it provides a glimpse into the minds and thought processes of the different writers. It's amazing to hear how they write and what motivated them to write the particular book being reviewed. This is an important point in that it's like peering through a window of a writer's mind and life, depending on how much they reveal, of course. I have heard many authors say that, and I'm paraphrasing, "If you are a serious writer, you do not write for anyone but yourself. All other opinions are meaningless." Inasmuch as you write to complete a book, you are the lone expert of your project. Celebration of completed steps and completed projects is essential. It is also up to the writer as how the celebration will occur and with whom.

I will offer this personal account as follows. After working on my first novel for years, with off and on starts, I finished my real first book as I sat on the screened porch of a vacation house on the Neuce River, in North Carolina. My wife had found this little gem of a place that provided the perfect place to write. The old farm house was situated on the banks of the river. I recall as I was writing, and as I started the next to the last chapter, finally encapsulating the ending of the story that had occupied a daily portion of my thinking for years, I began to feel the elation. And as I wrote the last paragraph, I called out to my wife, who had been supportive and patient with my efforts to finish the book. The moment that I typed the last word and hit enter after the last period, there was a moment of silent, inner elation. Then, I stood and walked into the den area where my wife was sitting. I announced that I had at last finished my book. We both jumped for joy. But it was a personal experience shared with my wife. There were no fireworks, no parties, just the personal and supportive celebration. I now had a completed first draft, the first major goal. Now the hard work begins…editing!

Celebrate your small but significant goals of writing! It will pay dividends.

Chapter 17

The Proofreading and Editing Process
By Candice W. N. Lawrence

After you've completed your manuscript, distanced yourself, and celebrated your accomplishment, it is time to revisit your hard work. Welcome to the editing and proofreading stages. In the editing stage, you will need to focus on things such a plot threads and consistency. During the proofreading stage, you will concentrate on finding any and all errors in your work. Some writers find these processes refreshing because they see how much their work has transformed; others find these processes long and tedious. It's important to set aside a few days between writing and reviewing your work because you are more likely to catch mistakes with a fresh mind than with a drained, I'm-finally-finished mindset. It may also help to divide your editing and proofreading stages into a few days, designating certain sections for certain times.

Another strategy that some writers find helpful during both of these processes is to print your work or type it. If you have written the manuscript by hand, take the time to type it onto the computer; if it is already typed, print it out and make comments or handwrite your drafts. This will force you to stop and think about everything you write or type. The more you slow down, the easier it will be to notice and correct errors throughout your manuscript.

If you're like me, and you color-code and make countless notes throughout your documents while you are writing, you'll want to pay special attention to these markings during the editing process. Occasionally, this method may lead you to develop new threads for the plot or discover any forgotten threads that have not been fully woven into the story. Sometimes these markings are signs or reminders that several paragraphs need to be shifted three chapters later or that a scene needs to be completely deleted. While it may be tempting to delete all comments after finishing a draft, it is crucial to carefully consider each one and to ensure that all comments and highlights are ultimately deleted for the final draft.

Moreover, the editing process shifts more of the focus on content instead of grammar and mechanics. During this stage, you want to concentrate on details—big and small details. This is key for consistency and continuity. As you read, make separate notes or charts to keep track of when certain characters are introduced and when certain information is revealed, as well as whom the information is revealed to. Refer to this information frequently as you read the text to ensure there are no repeated scenes, that every character is where he or she is supposed to be, and the right information is divulged at the right time. This is also a great opportunity to read for different elements such as dialogue and setting. Try concentrating on the dialogue to make sure the characters are true to themselves or to make sure the dialect is consistent, if applicable. Also, verify that a scene does not inexplicably shift between settings or geographical locations. Think about minor threads that you introduced early on; are they still present or relevant? As you edit, examine and document all of these aspects and more to avoid omitting pivotal information or disclosing revelations too soon.

Finally, there are several critical techniques to employ during the proofreading process. Even though it may sound strange to hear yourself, read your work aloud. I learned this strategy while working in Columbus State University's writing center and it has paid off tremendously. To this day, I read aloud everything I write. For a book-length work, I recommend reading each chapter aloud as you write—and then have a final review after you have finished writing the manuscript. Often, when we read our work aloud, we notice more mistakes or missed opportunities than we would have had we simply read over the work silently. Furthermore, there are lasting benefits outside of catching mistakes; you begin to recognize your own voice, rhythm (sentence length, diction, syntax, etc.), and style. If you feel uncomfortable reading your work aloud, try reading it to a trusted friend or family member—keep in mind, you do not have to ask for a critique at this stage, you're merely reading your work to them to help you proofread. You may also want to consider downloading text-to-speech software such as Read-

Please to hear your work read aloud while you take notes or make changes. After learning about this program from a friend, I have used it several times to note word choice and rhythm.

Once you find grammatical or mechanical mistakes (or as you are looking for them), don't simply rely on spell check—while it often highlights errors, there have been instances where it points out something that is not an error or overlooks an error. As an added precaution, grab a dictionary such as Merriam-Webster's or check out The Oxford English Dictionary (OED). If you are still uncertain about word choice, compare the dictionary entries and usage examples to be sure you are using or spelling the appropriate word. In the event that you are unable to find the word you are looking for, pick up a thesaurus to replace the troublesome word with a synonym.

Dictionaries and thesauri are not the only sources you should reference during the editing and proofreading stages, style manuals such as *The Elements of Style* by Strunk and White and the *Chicago Manual of Style* are also extremely beneficial. These texts, and others like them, explain things from grammar to formatting. If you are planning to publish via the traditional route, check to see what the publishing house's preferred style or format is—more on this later, though.

While some writers proofread and edit their drafts along the way, it is still a good idea to take a break from your completed drafts then return to do final revisions and proofread through to make sure you've caught all the overlooked mistakes. Whether you decide to combine the editing and proofreading stages (as some writers do when pressed for time or on a deadline), it is essential to be meticulous and observant in making changes or corrections.

Chapter 18

The Art of Writing a Good Sentence

When asked about telling yarns and writing his stories, Mark Twain once said, "Get your facts first, then you can distort them as you please." So is it with writing a well-constructed, attention getting sentence. In his book, *How to Write a Sentence*, Stanley Fish makes the point that at first content does not count. Fish further illustrates that in order to compose sentences that capture the reader, "content must take a backseat" (p.25). Stanley Fish declares that in order to understand how to write a "good" sentence, the sentence must be void of content, strip of any influence of context. There are the basics of writing sentences, such as subject verb agreement, use of adjectives and adverbs, selection of verbs, avoidance of the passive voice, and on and on. If you need a refresher course, there are hundreds of references and blogs on the internet that will assist anyone with improving the grammar and style of their writing. I prefer to attack this point from a variety of ways, from referencing the book on grammar, *The Elements of Style*, by Strunk and White, as well as other sources. I have been known to delve back into my high school English grammar textbook (*Writing with a Purpose* by McCrimmon, Fourth Edition) or Stephen King's "Toolbox" from his book entitled, *On Writing, a Memoir of a Craft* as he proclaims that a person who has decided to dive into the world of writing must be loosened and freed from the bonds of fear and constraint, both of which may have affected our ability to produce meaningful and imaginative narratives. Writing without constraints or fear of getting it incorrect the first time is a gift of realistic actualization. There is time for the edits. Walter Mosley's book, *This Year You Write Your Novel*, which I highly recommend as a keeper, stated that many writers and teachers spend so much time comparing their writing to that of past masters that they lose the "contemporary voice of the novel being created on this day," (p.11). One will not become a writer, he exclaims, "by aping the tones and phrases, form and content, of great books of the past." Both of these authors noted here and the books cited are essential for anyone who has begun their travels down the road as a writer or novelist.

My advice to anyone starting this process is to take an assessment of your writing skills. Know your weaknesses in the area of grammar. Set a plan of action to study and improve your level of understanding. But above all, write, write, write. If you don't have a writing coach, become one. Just like learning a new play at football practice. Break down the play. Identify the moves…blocking assignments…elements of writing and grammar that you need to learn and apply. Just as in football, you will not master the plays until you practice running them, you must put in the time with your writing. Don't let the fear of failure slow you down.

Stephen King knows how to deal with fear. "I'm convinced," he once stated, "that fear is at the root of most bad writing. . . . Good writing is often about letting go of fear and affectation."

If you have a thought and an imagination for a story, begin with short and concise sentences about the specific elements of the story. Use the exercise of writing ten sentences that chronologically describe the story, event, or scene you imagined. Avoid fluff and meaningless words. As Hemingway stated in an interview, "Don't write about an emotion, make it." In other words, use sentence structure and word choice to create that scene, that action, and deliver the reader what you have imagined in your mind. In *Screenplay: The Foundations for Screenwriters,* Syd Field explains that when writing a scene in a screen play, the writer must invoke the reader's mental capacity to not just imagine, but actually feel the emotions in the scene. He writes, "Reading a screenplay is like reading a novel, play, or article in the Sunday paper…I read the words on the page slowly, drinking in all the visual descriptions, nuances, and dramatic situations," (p.20). Syd Field's depiction of what he has read in a screenplay denotes the intensity delivered by the sentences used by the writer.

I do believe that some people learn better by observing a skill or form of art being done, and then later, practicing the skill or art until it has been mastered to some degree or level. I am one of those people. As a teacher for 28 years, I have taught students of all ages who learn in this same way. So as you are reading this chapter, here is an assignment: Go find a copy of the book titled *The Horse Whisperer* by Nicholas Evans. It was his first novel, which was later turned into a successful movie whereby Robert Redford played the lead role. Get this book and read the first chapter. It will grab you. It will rip your imagination from whatever chair or sofa you happen to be sitting. The details described in the first chapter set the tone for the entire book, as it also accomplished in the movie. Once you have read it and allowed some time to pass while you absorb the scene in your head, go back and examine the sentences in the scenes that lead up to the tragedy involving the girl and her horse. Study those sentences.

Hemingway weaved his own experiences from around the world into his stories. His protagonist characters' behavior and experiences mirrored his own affairs and indignations all around the world, from Paris to Africa to Havana. Hemingway used simple but powerful sentences and words that captured the imagination of his readers as well as his critics.

Write with clarity. Write with conciseness, forcefulness, correctness and with polished details. Write with purpose and passion.

Remember, there is always time to edit. Just write it.

Chapter 19

Using conflict and suspense to hook the reader:

When writing a fictional novel or short story, one sure fire way to peak reader interest is by creating conflict. How is this accomplished? Writing a novel is usually done by a story from a particular point of view, or perhaps more than one point of view. The storyline, including any conflict or suspense, etc., is carried by the use of dialogue. Hemingway was a master craftsman with the art of weaving a story into a tapestry of suspense, descriptive details, exposing of his character's flaws and by creating tension between the different characters around various points in his story. With all fictional stories, the writer has an end on mind. Sometimes when writing the story itself takes over the direction of the narrative. It takes on a life of its own because it is a work of art, being created in the mind of the writer.

In my view, there are three basic principles for successful fiction. Every successful novel will hold the reader's attention with suspense of conflict. Therefore, every good piece of fiction must have suspense, intrigue and wild imaginative elements to the details and descriptions of the plot twists and turns. These elements of suspense and conflict represent one of the three principles for good fiction writing. With this element, Agatha Christie comes to mind. She had an enormous career of writing books and stories that were in the suspense thriller/crime novel genre. She was a master at creating a story that utilized the elements of suspense and intrigue. Go to your local library and check-out a copy of any of her books. *Murder on the Orient Express,* written by Agatha Christie, is a solid example of the element of suspense used to frame the multiple plots and sub-plots in the story. Johnathan Kellerman is another author who is a master at using the elements of suspense and conflict to frame the story. In most all of Kellerman's books, the element of complex plots and subplots are used like a hall of mirrors in at the county fair to confuse and hide the twists and turns of each character and their flaws and intentions. Kellerman's background and training as a psychiatrist no doubt has provided him with an endless supply of ideas and storylines. And of course, the king of all suspense stories and novels is Stephen King. His books are surrounded and based on suspense and conflict. The plots draw the reader into the story and suddenly as they jump out of their skin and look up, hours have flown by and they're on page 396.

The second basic element of good fiction writing is Chaos. Within the first few pages, or at least by the end of the first chapter, depending on the story, the writer must create a very descriptive, destructive chaotic scene worthy of ratcheting up the intensity level of the reader to knuckle-biting level.

This is a deal breaker element. The writer has to hook the reader and cause the reader's sense of urgency and that emphatic sense of having to know the outcome. It is essential. Find a copy of The Horse Whisperer, by Nicholas Evans. Read only the part through the scene of the accident, and then, close the book, place on the table and envision what might come next (assuming you haven't read this book), and immediately check your physiological state. How tense are you? What thoughts are racing through your mind? What is your first impulse? All these questions represent what a reader experiences when he or she read a book that grabs them early and doesn't let go. They can't put the book down. I have known friends and relatives who will read almost continuously until they finish the book, if it grabs them. Their attention and intention are intense. This is where you want your book to land, right in the middle of the chaos, suspense and intensity of the given scene.

The third basic element to good fiction writing is, as the writer, not to become too eager to reveal the ending elements of the story too soon. As writers, we have to develop a discipline that is applied to the writing process. Remember you are creating a piece of narrative art. Time is on your side and you are the expert. You also, in most cases, know the ending. Don't reveal the ending too soon, or the reader will be lost and your book tossed in the basket to be taken the local church, homeless shelter or Goodwill Store. (And there's absolutely nothing wrong or indigent about any of the three mentioned) Your goal as a writer is to create you story, first and foremost; then, create a following, a readership.

There are many authors for whom people follow and read every word the author produces. I have my own list of writers that I follow and read on a regular basis. It's my escape, which is what books should do. I once read, while conducting some general research about writing a first novel, that the writer or author doesn't have to reveal every answer or solve every mystery or conflict. In fact, as a writer, if you leave some elements on the table for later, it can be addressed in the sequel. It also allows for the reader's curiosity to simmer over the possible answers and resolutions. This is what all good writers do. They leave the reader wanting more.

As writer, plan for the twists and turns of suspense and conflict. Create that explosive and chaotic scene that abruptly changes the direction of the storyline. Tease the reader with snippets of detail, only to pull back the reveal until later. Take the reader on wide goose chases down roads that only lead to a single clue. Use dialogue, as Hemingway did in his book *To Have and have Not,* where the story was buried in the details of the relationship between the couple. Imagine yourself having the conversation with your characters. Place yourself mentally there. Play out the scene in your mind. Then write it, full bore. Leave nothing out. Afterwards, allow the writing to sit for a time, minutes, hours, days, but give it some time. Then, go back and review it; read it and re-write it and leave the resolution elements out. Redirect the dialogue. Change the description of the scenes. Change the temperament of one character's dialogue to another. And save the reveal and resolution until the last moment in the book. It will be exhilarating for you as the writer, and will keep the reader coming back for more. Write with confidence. Think about the direction of the story constantly and look for strategies and mechanisms in which to frame or direct the story and plot.

Getting Published!

The following chapters in this section will focus on the processes of getting your book published, and the options that now exist in the marketplace.

Chapter 20

POD Publishing vs. the Traditional Route

I am writing this chapter assuming that you are now ready to begin thinking of how to publish your book and which option to choose. I will provide you with a description of your options, but I strongly that you go ahead now and purchase the book by Morris Rosenthal titled *Book Publishing: Print-On-Demand.* This is the only book you will need. Read it and keep it on your bedside table, desk or in your briefcase.

The self-publishing business has become a multi-billion dollar industry. Yes, you read it correctly. In years past, there was only one option for a writer to become a published author, aside from the university print shops and publishing apprentices, one had to spend years as a starving artist, writing for minimum wages in hopes of finding an agent that would accept his book. There are stories upon stories where authors spent years being rejected before getting their first break, only to earn a meager amount of royalties, while the publishing company reaped the bounty. The publishing world is different now!

Self-publishing has become the segue into the publishing world. While there are still traditional publishing companies, the choice of self-publishing increases each year. Pick up any writer's magazine at your local bookstore, and you will find articles, workshops, and various self-publishing companies advertising for self-published books. Some even offer editing services, formatting, and other services related to publishing or printing your book. The formula and difference is as follows: The traditional "big" publisher will own the rights to your book, unless you are a big time author, and will promote and market your book. They take all the risks, invest time and money in the marketing, printing and distribution of your book, and in return, you earn a small royalty to the tune of 2 to 12 percent per book.

The self-publishing route provides the author with more options and more control, and a bigger royalty. This route requires the cost of formatting and printing be paid up front. The cost will vary depending on which company you select. In return, you, as the author, set the price for your book, get a larger royalty from the sales of your book, and have complete control over the marketing and sales of your book. The options are completely at your command, as long as you understand that unless you do the marketing, you will not sell any books.

In my opinion, the self-publishing option is the best and only option for many or most beginning authors. However, it is pure American entrepreneurship. And you are in good company. Benjamin Franklin self-published his books, as did Walt Whitman.

The following will blow your mind. I hope it will convince you that self-publishing is a viable and legitimate route and option for most authors.

FAMOUS SELF-PUBLISHED BOOKS:

Remembrance of things Past, by Marcel Proust
Ulysses, by James Joyce
The Adventures of Peter Rabbit, by Beatrix Potter
The Wealthy Barber, by David Chilton
The Bridges of Madison County
What Color is Your Parachute?
In Search of Excellence by Tom Peters
The Celestine Prophecy by James Redfield
The Elements of Style by William Strunk, Jr. (and his student E. B. White)
The Joy of Cooking
When I Am an Old Woman I Shall Wear Purple
Life's Little Instruction Book
Robert's Rules of Order

OTHER FAMOUS AUTHORS WHO SELF-PUBLISHED

Deepak Chopra
Gertrude Stein
Zane Grey
Upton Sinclair
Carl Sandburg
Ezra Pound
Mark Twain
Edgar Rice Burroughs
Stephen Crane

Bernard Shaw
Anais Nin
Thomas Paine
Virginia Wolff
E.E. Cummings
Edgar Allen Poe
Rudyard Kipling
Henry David Thoreau
Benjamin Franklin
Walt Whitman
Alexandre Dumas
William E.B. DuBois
Beatrix Potter

REJECTED BY PUBLISHERS

Kathryn Sockett - The Help - 60 times
Pearl S. Buck - The Good Earth - 14 times
Norman Mailer - The Naked and the Dead - 12 times
Patrick Dennis- Auntie Mame - 15 times
George Orwell - Animal Farm
Richard Bach - Jonathan Livingston Seagull - 20 times
Joseph Heller - Catch-22 - 22 times (!)
Mary Higgins Clark - first short story - 40 times
Alex Haley - before Roots - 200 rejections
Robert Persig - Zen and the Art of Motorcycle Maintenance - 121 times
John Grisham - A Time to Kill - 15 publishers and 30 agents (he ended up publishing it himself)
Chicken Soup for the Soul - 33 times
Dr. Seuss - 24 times
Louis L'Amour - 200 rejections

Jack London - 600 before his first story
John Creasy - 774 rejections before selling his first story. He went on to write 564 books, using fourteen names.
Jerzy Kosinski - 13 agents and 14 publishers rejected his best-selling novel when he submitted it under a different name, including Random House, which had originally published it.
Diary of Anne Frank
During his entire lifetime, Herman Melville's timeless classic, Moby Dick, sold only 3,715 copies.

(Thanks to Dan Poynter's website for this info; see www.parapublishing.com)

****

I included the aforementioned to demonstrate that self-publishing is not a new option to publishing nor it is a bad option. Know your options. Know your entrepreneurial power.

The thing you must master, unless you have plenty of green backs to dole out, is the art of editing and formatting. Or, you must have options or partners that have those skills, or be willing to pay for that to be done. The published product must be enticing to read, possess an intriguing story and must be nicely formatted and have a minimum or zero typos or errors. Every article, book, or interview you hear or read will fore warn you to edit, edit, edit, and then, edit again. In the end, you will not regret it.

Chapter 21

Marketing your book

How many of you reading this chapter had a mom who sold some type of product, whether it was Tupperware, jewelry, May Kay Cosmetics, copper housewares, or perhaps pictorial church directories? If so, you'll remember the never ending list of people, friends and family, who would be called with an announcement of a party at your house. Or, perhaps, an up and coming star salesperson would host the party in return for her starter set of merchandise. Selling one's product is a time endured practice.

When I lived and worked in Texas, I learned about how large cattle ranches operate. The cattle ranchers raise very specific herds; protect the lineage of the bulls used for breeding, and look forward to the cattle sales each year. It's all about raising a superior product and getting the product to market. A good friend of mine in Alabama also raises cattle, but on a smaller scale than a big Texas cattle ranch. He once remarked that every time a calf drops, it means potentially more money toward his annual revenues. As much as he enjoys the outdoors, riding around on his tractor, it's a business where every calf counts, and it's about the end product. The same is with marketing and selling your book.

Here's a warning: Be mindful, very mindful with what you choose to read and to whom you choose to listen about the aspects of marketing your book.

Marketing your book is as pure and basic as it comes. It is pure entrepreneurial spirit. It is all about you as the creator of this product, getting out there, making contacts, working or establishing your network and putting your book out there. It takes courage. It takes guts. It requires a layer of tough skin when the criticisms fly. But the bottom line is this: It takes you, the author; convincing people they need and should purchase your book. Now, how is this accomplished?

The Product

Say your book has been written, edited and published through the self-publishing method of your choice, either through your own efforts and company or through another reputable self-publishing company. The book cover is outstanding and attractive. During the cover selection process, your book cover was vetted and designed by someone or a company who specializes in book-cover designs.

The book is on a great topic, one that is bound to attract interest once it is presented. The book is written with a specific audience in mind, whether the audience is from a wide social spectrum or a specific genre or topic area. Regardless, the book is tight, readable, interesting and even imaginative.

Marketing Resources

As your book nears completion of the publishing/printing process, it is recommended that your first order include at least 100 to perhaps 150 copies for your personal quick access. These copies will be needed for book signings, booking signing parties and for use as complimentary signed copies to special people.

Order the same number of marketing postcards that have the book cover on one side and a place for you to mail to each person on your marketing list. You will need to replenish your supply of books and cards if sales become brisk.

Next, order 250 to 500 business cards depicting the book cover, your name and an email or webpage address. You will also need to set-up a webpage solely for marketing your book, as well as set-up a business email where inquiries come directly to your inbox. Also, set-up a pay-pal account and a pay-pal purchase button on your website where interested persons may actually purchase a copy or copies of your book. The money drops into a designated account and an email notifies you that someone has made a purchase. You then deliver on the purchase by mailing out a signed copy.

Once these purchasing mechanisms have been put into place and are operable, you may go to the next phase. I recommend placing an order or having a friend place an order to verify that the system works properly.

The Book Signing Party

Everyone loves a party where friends gather, eat, drink and celebrate an accomplishment. Hopefully, you have enough close friends and acquaintances where someone close to you will take on the task of organizing a book party. This would ordinarily occur in the evening, and perhaps on a weekend. Be mindful of sports games scheduled so that you don't run into any scheduling conflicts. Your friends and their friends will likely choose a football game over a book signing party.

Early into the party, when it can be determined that most who are expected to actually show are present, have your host get everyone's attention, thank everyone for coming, wish them well and much enjoyment with the food and merriment. Then, your host should announce the reason for the party, although everyone knows, right; next an introduction of the book and yourself as the author. Thank everyone for coming. Make a brief statement about the book and gently direct your guests to where the books are situated. Have several in a stack on various tables, all signed, numbered and dated. Have a bowl or decorative jar adjacent the stacks of books for those who purchase a copy. As a party treat, set-up an old typewriter for guests to type you a note of thanks, encouragement or an I.O.U. This idea is used by many brides at their reception where guests are able to type a personal note of congratulations. It always peaks everyone's interest, and you may found yourself running out of books.

The Marketing List

Everyone in sales has developed and used a marketing list. It begins with what is called your "warm market." When you have your best thinking and focus time, sit down and time yourself with writing a list of 100 people you know, no matter how well, just write the names on a list. Time yourself with two minute intervals. After the first two minutes, think again for a few minutes and start list number two. Approach this exercise in this way. If you had a new child and wanted everyone you knew to know, who would be on your list? Take the same approach and make your list. If you're lucky, your list will consist of more than 100, even more than two hundred. You now have your first marketing list.

Remember to get your supply of postcards and business cards with the picture of your book on it. This will prove crucial.

Take your list and develop it one step further. Research, look-up or whatever you have to do to get the current address, telephone numbers and email of the people on your list. In this day and age, many of the people on your list may also be your friends on social media. A word of caution here: Not everyone receives well any advertisements on their Facebook pages or Twitter accounts. Instead, create your own Facebook page for your book and post it on your status page. Invite your FB friends and family to take a look. This way it doesn't encroach on their time or personal space, and they control the point and pace of access.

Keep your newly developed list aside for now. The next task is to contact any and all independent book stores, coffee shops, or anyone you might know who has or manages a small business in your area. Do not call them, but make a personal visit and take some copies of your book.

Go into the business and ask if you could have five minutes of their time. Ask if they will allow you to set-up and advertise a book signing at their place of business. You'll do all the advertising and getting the word out, which means they get free advertising as well. You'll be as non-intrusive as possible, and it will be great for both you and him or her as the business owner or manager. Also, be mindful of going to big name bookstores of coffee shops, whose names I will purposely omit. They are your corporately owned establishments, and while they have their good points, you need to market and sell your book. These shops may sometimes turn a blind eye and deaf ear to any "indie" - independent sellers, writers and publishers.

Divide your list in chunks of 15 to 25 people. Contact them by phone or in person, which face-to-face is always best. As you get book signings scheduled, make calls and/or visits to the people on your list. Personally invite them to your book signing. Offer free copies if they bring a couple of friends or extra folks. People always like something for free.

Follow-up your personal invitations with a postcard announcing when and where, as well as a handwritten thank you note. Make it meaningful and connect with the person. Personalize each one so that each is different and unique. Keep up with your list as they will be a source of referrals down the road.

The day of the first book signing will be filled with nervousness and anxiety. It's normal. Soak it all in, it's worth it and it will be exciting. Wear a contagious smile and have plenty of pens ready for the signing. Also, use your postcards to write thank you notes to those who attended. Do this the next day and mail them out right away.

Repeat the afore-described steps with your entire list. Then write a new list of new people and begin again. This should generate many books to be sold.

Also, if you have not already, purchase the following book: *Book Publishing: Print-On-Demand,* written by Morris Rosenthal. Available online only.

Now, it's time to write the sequel.

Chapter 22

An LLC or Limited Liability Corporation ~~ for Publishing, Marketing and Writer Research

Why an LLC is necessary for writing, publishing, marketing, or conducting book research, one might ask? The answer is not as complicated as one might think.

I will follow the trend of this book and keep this to the point and brief. Simply stated; if one chooses to embark on the journey of writing, publishing and marketing a book, and if it is done from the perspective of a small business, then one would be prudent to become well versed in the tax laws and regulations in order to simply position oneself to best advantage, as permitted by the tax laws and regulations, per the I.R.S. It is also advisable to seek advice and counsel from a professional tax accountant, tax or small business attorney or both, and set up an LLC for the purpose of positioning oneself from a business advantage, but also for protecting oneself as an author and writer. Although a disclaimer will appear within the first few pages of the book that the book as a piece of fiction is the sole and total creation of its author and has no bearing or resemblance from anyone or any persons known or unknown to the author. Get the business end of writing, publishing and marketing your book in order soon after you have begun the research and writing process. It may prove to be a big tax advantage as you labor by day and research and write by nights and weekends. This may be considered the science behind the work as a writer and publisher. Get your business affairs in line and set-up, quickly.

Chapter 23

A Final Word

So you've finished reading this compilation of information, advice and vignettes, and you might be asking, "Where's the *Southern Twist*?" Fair enough.

The *Southern Twist*, as it were, is with the art of storytelling. Whether you're a song writer, singer, a poet or a newly discovered author of fiction, the art of storytelling is a must. Think about the family gatherings around special events, like Thanksgiving or Christmas, when people gather to share stories about their lives, swap details and gossip from wherever they live, and all eventually delve into the memories of times and stories gone by. It's mesmerizing. As they pull their chairs up to the circle or in the room or on the screened porch, the tales and yarns begin to unfurl. Think about it. This is what you want to accomplish, in part, with your book. Close your eyes and visualize yourself there, right in the middle with your head turning left and right, trying to keep up with the hooks, crooks and turns of the tales and yarns. Now go write your book.

As for the technical aspect of this book, I hope it wasn't disappointing. If you need help writing good sentences, seek out those resources, get focused and start writing. My partner with this project is a very gifted and talented young lady whose experiences and training will bode well for her future. She has an eye for detail and understands the meaning and importance of the underlying foundations, emotions and personal history that plays into the creation of every story, whether written or passed down through oral history. When asked about how one writes a novel, many authors have simply said, "If you have an idea about a book, get a computer or a pad and pencil, and write." Their advice cannot be more direct and to the point. Muster your courage and go write. Don't worry about grammar, sentence structure or even details of the story; just begin your writing process. Like a car that's running a little rough, a good tune-up, a good car wash, and some "new car" fragrance will make it run, look and sound great. Same with your writing; once you get your ideas down on paper, go have it tuned up and cleaned up. You'll be surprised how great your story will sound.

Candice Lawrence and I, as the authors and creators of this little book on writing and publishing a novel, have attempted to give you enough information to launch your new project. There are tons and tons of information on how to write and how to get published. Be careful not to overwhelm your brain as you shift through the mountains of information. Every new author and every new book will proclaim to have all the secret formulas. Here's the secret:

There are no secret formulas! Writing requires hard work, incredibly focused attention, and a belief that you can write your book. I believe you can!

The following are some rules of writing by Elmore Leonard, who died in 2013. He was a renowned playwright, noted author and lecturer, and was considered to be the "father" of the screenwriter's genre. The books on writing screenplays are still to this day considered to be the utmost authority of all written books or articles. He was an incredibly, talented man, who came from humble beginnings, which is my point. He wrote his first books while selling insurance until he was asking to take days off from work so much that he finally realized that he had hit the big time. So, he resigned his job as an insurance agent and began speaking, lecturing and of course, writing. He is sorely missed in the literary world. Read the expose' of an interview of him from 2012. The advice here is golden.

Elmore Leonard's Ultimate Guide for Would-Be Writers in Books, Literature, Writing | June 25th, 2012

"If it sounds like writing," says Elmore Leonard, "I rewrite it."

Leonard's writing sounds the way people talk. It rings true. In novels like *Get Shorty, Rum Punch* and *Out of Sight,* Leonard has established himself as a master stylist, and while his characters may be lowlifes, his books are received and admired in the highest circles.

In 1998, Martin Amis recalled visiting Saul Bellow and seeing Leonard's books on the old man's shelves. "Bellow and I agreed," said Amis, "that for an absolutely reliable and unstinting infusion of narrative pleasure in a prose miraculously purged of all false qualities, there was no one quite like Elmore Leonard."

In 2006 Leonard appeared on BBC Two's The Culture Show to talk about the craft of writing and give some advice to aspiring authors. In the program, shown above, Leonard talks about his deep appreciation of Ernest Hemingway's work in general, and about his particular debt to the 1970 crime novel The Friends of Eddie Coyle, by George V. Higgins. While explaining his approach, *Leonard jots down three tips*:

"You have to listen to your characters."

"Don't worry about what your mother thinks of your language."

"Try to get a rhythm."

"I always refer to style as sound," says Leonard as, "The sound of the writing." Some of Leonard's suggestions appeared in a 2001 New York Times article that became the basis of his 2007 book, *Elmore Leonard's 10 Rules of Writing*.

Here are those rules in outline form:

Never open a book with the weather.
Avoid prologues.
Never use a verb other than "said" to carry dialogue.
Never use an adverb to modify the verb "said."
Keep your exclamation points under control!
Never use the words "suddenly" or "all hell broke loose."
Use regional dialect, patois, sparingly.
Avoid detailed descriptions of characters;
same for places and things.
Leave out the parts readers tend to skip.

You can read more from Leonard on his rules in the 2001 *Times* article. And you can read his new short story, "Ice Man," in *The Atlantic*.

References, Footnotes and Acknowledgements

References for the writer, some of which have appeared as direct references in this publication.

(2007) Mosley, Walter. This Year You Write Your Novel; Little, Brown and Company
Hachette Book Group USA, New York, NY.

(2011) Fish, Stanley. How To Write a Sentence and How to read one. Harper Collins Books, New York, NY.

(2010) Leonard, Elmore. Elmore Leonard's Ten Rules of Writing. William Morrow. Harper Collins Press, New York, NY.

(1993) Hacker, Diane. A Pocket Style Manual. Charles H. Christensen, Publisher, St. Martin's Press, New York, NY.

(2000) King, Stephen. On Writing, A Memoir of the Craft. Scribner Publishing, New York, NY.

(2010) Ingermanson, Randy and Economy, Peter. Writing Fiction for Dummies. Wiley Publishing, Inc., Hoboken, N.J.

(1967) McCrimmon, James. Writing with a Purpose. Houghton Mifflin Company, 4th Edition, New York, NY.

(2012) Aiken, Ronald. Death Has Its Benefits. Nightbird Publishing, Norcross, GA.

(2009) Liu, Eric and Noppe-Brandon, Scott. Imagination first. Josey-Bass, San Francisco, CA.

(2008) Rosenthal, Morris. Book Publishing: Print-On-Demand. Foner Books, Springfield, MA.

(2010) Ingermanson, Randy, and Economy, Peter. Writing Fiction for Dummies.Wiley Publushing, Inc. Hoboken, N.J.

(2002) White, Nancy. Writing Power. Kaplan Publishing, New York, NY.

(2012) Elmore Leonard's Ultimate Guide for Would-Be Writers in Books, Literature, Writing | June 25th, 2012

(2010) Block, Lawrence. Writing the Novel: From Plot to Print. Open Road, Integrated Media, New York, NY

~About the Author~

Candice Lawrence

Candice W. N. Lawrence was born in Savannah, Georgia. She grew up playing instrumental music with her older brother, but discovered her love for writing by the age of fifteen. Lawrence spent most of her life attending performing arts schools in which she focused on music and creative writing. She credits *Jane Eyre* as the novel that made her choose to seriously pursue writing.

Lawrence graduated from Columbus State University in Columbus, Georgia, where she earned her BA in English Language and Literature with a concentration in Creative Writing. While in college, she studied abroad in England, tutored, wrote and edited for several publications including her own compilation of short stories and Honors Thesis on Southern Fiction. She is also a graduate of the University of Denver's Publishing Institute.

~About the Author~

Jesse R. Hale

Jesse R. (Randall) Hale was born in Bessemer, Alabama. He grew up in a rural area and community near the town of Bessemer, Alabama, during a time where one's imagination was a must. At the age of 12, Hale visited with relatives in California, which set in motion a desire to go and see what lie beyond the community of Hopewell, Alabama. As an adult, Hale traveled for a time extensively in the Caribbean, visiting several islands over a period of time, made several trips to Mexico and Central America, and has traveled extensively in many parts of the western United States.

Among the authors and writers admired and revered by Hale include Mark Twain, William Faulkner, Ernest Hemingway, Elmore Leonard, and many other modern era writers and authors.

Hale has spent the last 28 years as an educator, serving in the roles of teacher, coach and administrator. Prior to entering the field of education, Hale worked in the concrete industry, operating concrete plants in Alabama, Louisiana and Texas. Throughout his life experiences, the people and characters, places and situations, have all contributed to his sources of imagination and experiences for writing and authorship.

~ Notes ~

~ Notes ~

www.ingramcontent.com/pod-product-compliance
Lightning Source LLC
LaVergne TN
LVHW021520080426
835509LV00018B/2576

9780983837671